Sean Kenney's Art with LEGO® Bricks

Building
Amazing
Creations

Sean Kenney

Building Amazing Creations

Sean Kenney's Art
with LEGO® Bricks

Christy Ottaviano Books

Henry Holt and Company • New York

*For Jung Ah, Geoffrey,
and everyone on my team for
making possible all the amazing
work we've done over the years*

I would like to thank Christy Ottaviano, Elynn Cohen,
Patrick Collins, Jessica Anderson, Melinda Ackell, and John Nora
for all their help in the making of this book.

Henry Holt and Company, *Publishers since 1866*
Henry Holt® is a registered trademark of Macmillan Publishing Group, LLC
175 Fifth Avenue, New York, NY 10010 • mackids.com

Library of Congress Cataloging-in-Publication Data
Names: Kenney, Sean, author.
Title: Building amazing creations : Sean Kenney's art with LEGO bricks / Sean Kenney.
Other titles: Art with LEGO bricks
Description: New York : Henry Holt and Company, 2017 | Audience: Age 7–18.
Identifiers: LCCN 2017009637 | ISBN 9781627790185 (hardcover)
Subjects: LCSH: Models and modelmaking—Juvenile literature. | LEGO
toys—Juvenile literature. | Plastic sculpture—Juvenile literature.
Classification: LCC TT154 .K44 2017 | DDC 745.5928—dc23
LC record available at https://lccn.loc.gov/2017009637

Our books may be purchased in bulk for promotional, educational, or business use. Please
contact your local bookseller or the Macmillan Corporate and Premium Sales Department at
(800) 221-7945 ext. 5442 or by e-mail at MacmillanSpecialMarkets@macmillan.com.

First edition, 2017 / Designed by Elynn Cohen
Printed in China by RR Donnelley Asia Printing Solutions Ltd., Dongguan City, Guangdong Province

1 3 5 7 9 10 8 6 4 2

CONTENTS

INTRODUCTION

Several years ago I came across an insightful quote in a book by Louis Nizer, noted lawyer and author, artist, lecturer, and advisor to some of the most powerful people in the world. He said, "A man who works with his hands is a laborer. A man who works with his hands and his brain is a craftsman. But a man who works with his hands, and his brain, and his heart . . . is an artist." I think about this quote nearly every day. Am I an artist or a craftsman? How can I give a spark of energy to everything that I create? How can I make a sculpture come alive? How can I make you feel what my sculpture is feeling? How can I infuse myself into my work? These are the kinds of questions I ask myself whenever I am creating something new.

After working for ten years in an office as a web designer, I realized the corporate world wasn't for me so I quit my job and opened my own art studio in New York City. In everything that I do, I strive to make my creations more than simply a stack of pieces pushed together the right way. I want my work to be elegant and visually pleasing. Often I struggle to balance the physical presence of large sculptures with the delicacy of their natural forms. I pore over photos to make sure that I capture every detail of my subject, whether it's a skyscraper or a bumblebee. In the case of living creatures, I watch countless videos and observe how they behave in the wild, how they interact with one another, and how they nurture their young. I aim to imbue the eyes of every creature I create with life—so that for a second, you think you're looking at the real thing.

Over the past fifteen years, I've discovered that I have a distinct visual style and that I shouldn't be afraid to impress my style onto my work. I now create sculptures, portraits, models, and contemporary art for people of all ages and for television and major corporations. My exhibits have traveled all around the United States and have gone as far as South America, Europe, Australia, and Asia.

I believe that every person is born with the urge to create. Ideas feed into new ideas in an endless cycle of creative growth. I hope you enjoy the Amazing Creations that I've featured in this book. But more important, I hope the creations in this book inspire you to create some great models of your own.

Sean Kenney

Building as a kid

Sean and some of his team: Sean Kenney, Meghan Ritchey, Geoffrey Miller, Luis Seda, Haksul Lee, Jung Ah Kim, Valerie Champagne, David Pagano, Natsuki Takauji

ANIMALS

ANIMALS

It's both rewarding and challenging to develop a creature with a personality, subtleties, and a story. I've created scores of animals—sculptures for my botanical garden exhibit, commissions of people's pets, and plenty of others just for fun. And they run the gamut from tiny to huge. The owl below is only two inches tall, but the fox is nearly six feet long and three times as large as a real fox! Can you tell what part I used for the green frog's eye? (Hint: It's normally on top of a Minifigure.)

This is the largest sculpture I've ever created. It weighs 625 pounds and contains more than 125,000 pieces.

Polar Bear Mother and Cubs

I was touched to learn about the relationship that a mother polar bear has with her cubs. She teaches them to hunt; together they have a very visible and strong love. Watching videos of polar bears with their cubs, I was taken by how almost-human they seemed. I wanted to capture this aspect of their lives.

 Peacock

This peacock is the most visually intricate piece I've ever created—and the second largest! Every feather is sculpted in place and gently layered atop the next, and thousands of little dips, pocks, and ridges create the illusion of quills and feathering. The sculpture weighs more than 100 pounds and is supported by a hidden metal armature that is custom-welded to precise dimensions so it fits perfectly between the pieces. Most of the model is only ½ inch to 2 inches thick. In all, it comprises 68,827 pieces and over 625 hours of work.

After the sculpture was finished, it left my Brooklyn studio for a crating facility to have the sculpture fitted for a custom foam-lined traveling exhibition crate.

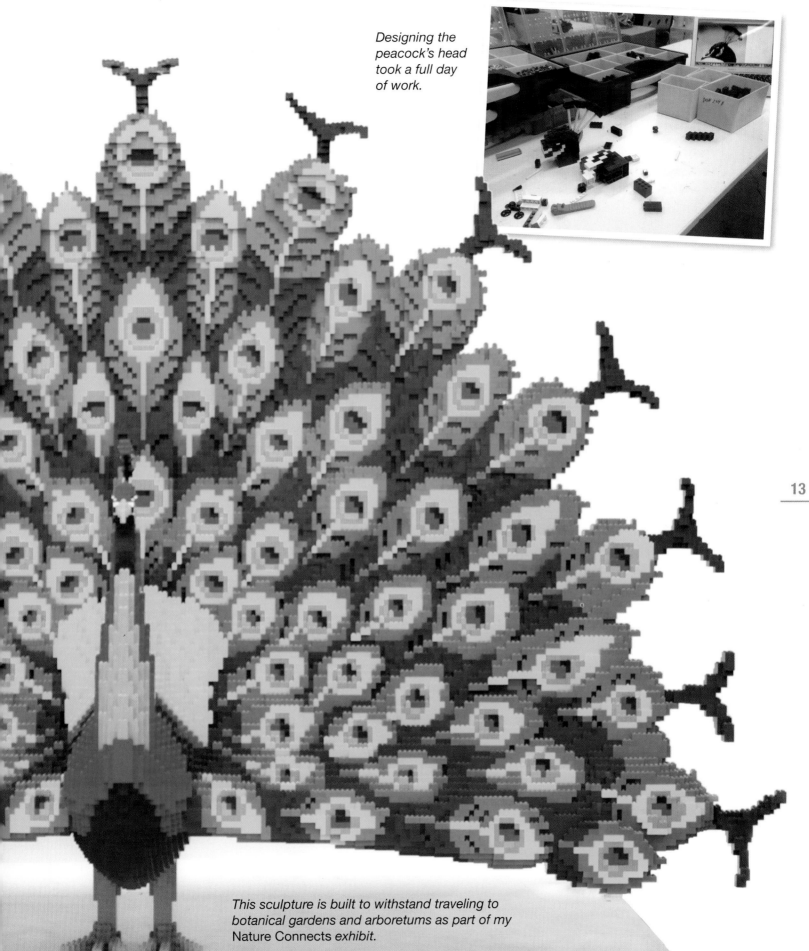

Designing the peacock's head took a full day of work.

This sculpture is built to withstand traveling to botanical gardens and arboretums as part of my Nature Connects exhibit.

Rubber Ducky

Okay, rubber duckies aren't REAL animals, but this one's so cool! The giant sculpture has been in art shows and on TV—and even made a special appearance at a movie screening in New York City. My assistant Jung Ah gave him a hug while he was trying to hail a taxi.

Clown Fish

The models of Nemo and Marlin were created as a Christmas present for a friend with an aquarium of clown fish. Marlin is about eight inches long and contains about 600 pieces; Nemo is about six inches long and contains about 400 pieces. Because of their vertical black and white stripes, I had to build their bodies entirely sideways. Their faces are the only part of the models that were built in a standard "studs up" fashion.

16

 **Tiny Turtles**

These life-size diamondback terrapin turtles are each only a few inches long. They were installed at the Philadelphia Zoo as part of an exhibit that I created to bring attention to the plight of endangered animals.

The Duck Family

Daddy Duck leads his family for a walk, with one baby snug underneath. Wait, is that an egg with feet?

Gray Mouse

Squeak squeak whoosh!

Did you notice his nose is a pink space helmet?

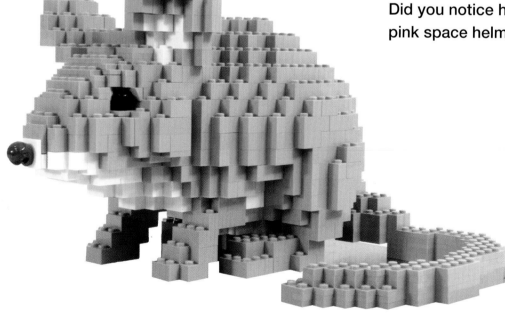

18

Puffer Fish

The tech company Bitly asked me to reimagine their two-dimensional cartoon puffer fish mascot as a three-dimensional sculpture. It now hangs proudly in their Manhattan headquarters.

Snake

With this creation, I wanted the overlapping coils of the snake's body to look creepy and somewhat menacing.

Birds vs. Squirrels

Who will be the first to consume all the bird food? Squirrels are always getting to the food inside bird feeders. This is one of my favorite sculptures because it's so silly and energetic.

In my mind, while the squirrels are running frenetically about to the theme song of *Mission: Impossible*, the birds are just sitting there saying, *"Sigh.* Not these guys again."

Did you notice what I used for bird food?

 Fox Hunting Rabbit

Not only do giant fox sculptures hunt rabbits, they also hunt Jung Ah. I've got the rabbit eating out of my hand (green pieces, anyway).

 # Mother and Baby Bison

This fuzzy mother is out for a walk in the plains with her little boy. . . .

Professor Meowingtons

Professor Meowingtons is the world-famous, Twittering, Facebooking, Internet-savvy pet of professional musician Deadmau5. This portrait loves shiny things and falls off the wall if you're carrying catnip.

Showing Outside

I'm posing these golden lion tamarins so that they'll look like they're interacting with one another and with their landscape the way real monkeys would. It's important to me that the sculptures I create look at home in their environment. Anyone can just plop a monkey sculpture in the grass, but I want them crawling through the trees, picking bugs out of one another's fur, playing with twigs and rocks, and other authentic details that help them appear more lifelike.

My outdoor sculptures have to be built extra sturdy to withstand wind, rain, ice, harsh sunlight, and physical abuse from real animals and falling branches through the years. The sculptures are assembled in my New York City art studio, then custom-fit in museum exhibition crates so they can be safely transported around the world. Once they arrive, a team of art handlers use forklifts and tools to get the sculptures installed and landscaped.

Acting Penguin-y

Before building these penguins, my team and I watched online videos of real penguins reacting to crowds at a zoo. We thought it was amazing that most of the time they just stood together looking at the same things.

These penguins were on display at the Philadelphia Zoo, Utah's Hogle Zoo, and Zoo Miami.

🧱 Care for a Swim?

How do you make a 150-pound, five-foot water platter float in a pond? How is that koi fish jumping up out of the water? I can't tell you all my secrets—you'll just have to guess!

This vibrant water scene has been installed in ponds, lakes, and water features at botanical gardens around the United States.

Mom, Dad, and Baby

As a father of two small children, I know what it's like to be a watchful dad who wants to protect his family.

I also know that the love a mother has for her baby is something very powerful and special. I'm sure deer feel the same way.

This three-foot-long Galápagos tortoise has a secret inside. . . . A tiny Mario is built into a chamber in his shell!

Squirrels have cute butts!

"Quick! Let's eat all this before Sean builds it into a cat!"

Goldfinches

These life-size American goldfinches are each about six inches long and are mounted to a real bird feeder. They were designed with multiple postures and set up to look as realistic as possible.

Even though they're the smallest model in my traveling exhibit *Nature Connects*, they're many a fan's favorite . . . often because people walk right past them, thinking they're real!

Target Bullseye

Global mega-retailer Target's mascot, "Bullseye," is a visual icon recognized by millions of people. This sculpture, commissioned by Target, was on display at Art Basel Miami Beach 2015 and on New York City's Chelsea art gallery scene. The sculpture stands 5.5 feet tall, contains 39,800 pieces, and took about two months to create.

I wanted Bullseye to look super friendly, like he was about to leap into your lap. (Although since he weighs over 200 pounds, you probably wouldn't want him to. . . .)

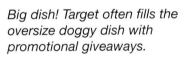

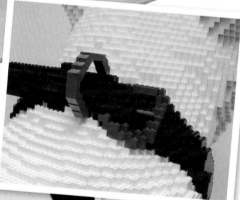

Big dish! Target often fills the oversize doggy dish with promotional giveaways.

N-ear-ly done, we put some pink pieces in place for Bullseye's inner ears.

Lion

This larger-than-life lion stands about five feet tall. I wanted him to appear regal, relaxed, and sophisticated. When we build sculptures like this, we search online through lots of photos and videos of actual lions to make the sculpture look as real as possible. My assistants Jisun and Geoffrey (bottom left and right) spent a lot of time working on the face, building and rebuilding it over and over to ensure the lion's expression was just right. Color, in particular, was tricky with the lion's eyes. We settled on a hard-to-find golden-colored radar dish as the iris of the eye. And for the whiskers, I used fiber-optic tubes that came in a spaceship set from the late 1990s. This sculpture is now part of the Denver Zoo's permanent collection.

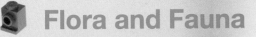

Flora and Fauna

My team and I spent five thousand hours creating the sculptures you see here, but just five minutes taking silly pictures.

43

ROBOTS

I love building science-fiction robots because I get the chance to imagine something that doesn't exist, and then decide how to build it.

I try to imagine what a world of robots without humans would be like: What kinds of jobs would the robots have? How would they be built to do their jobs? I imagine these robots would be half "person" and half "equipment"—for instance, a delivery person combined with a delivery truck becomes a Deliverybot.

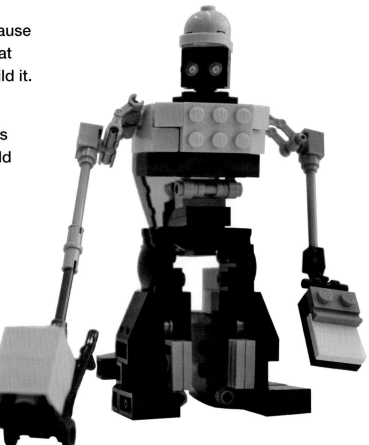

Mix-N-Matchbot doesn't care that his outfit doesn't match; he's just happy to have a bellyful of glowing orange energy.

Need anything cleaned? Broombot is here to help! Unfortunately, Dustpanbot is nowhere to be seen.

I love to take weird pieces and use them in nonstandard ways. This tan robot has gray barrels attached to a car wheel base for his shoulders. (And a pretty neat belly button.)

Robots come in all shapes and sizes. Why is this Firebot so tall? Turn the page to find out. . . .

🧱 Here, Kitty, Kitty!

Firebots need to help rescue cats stranded in trees. This tall robot can also reach up to put out fires in tall buildings, and he plays a mean game of botsketball.

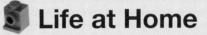 Life at Home

Even robots like to enjoy an afternoon at home. I'm not sure why they play video games on a console instead of just running them in their robo brains, or why they need a cuckoo clock if their brains have digital clocks. At least the couch hovers.

These are older prototypes of the bot family. Dad had a "bow tie," the boy was a different color, and the dog wasn't nearly as cute.

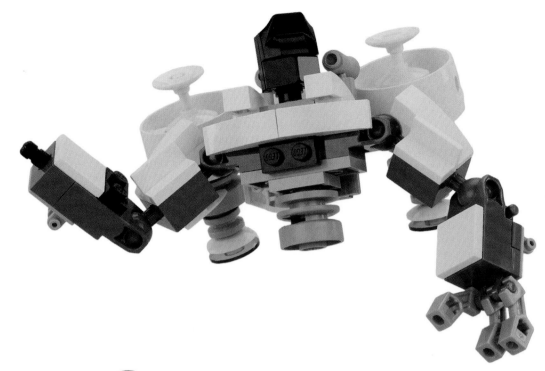

"Why So Angry, Mr. Robot?"

I grew up watching robot cartoons on TV in the 1980s, and came to think of robots as tough fighters with weapons, gridlocked in warring factions. Reflecting on this, I made these two tough bots. As I've gotten older, I've realized that fighting and shooting are pretty terrible things and found new inspiration in Atomic Age automation and retro styling—the idea that machines can make our lives better. You'll find that most of the robots in this chapter fit this latter perspective.

 # Giant Boybot

This giant robot is a scaled-up version of the little boybot standing at his feet. First I built each piece twelve times larger than normal, then combined them to make a robot twelve times larger than the original.

I originally designed this model so that I could light up the translucent eye pieces with LEDs located inside his body, but I never ended up adding them in.

🧱 Person + Machine = Bot on the Job

In creating all these construction robots, I tried to imagine what it would look like if different kinds of machinery became combined with the people who use them. How would the machine be remade to be part of the body of the robot?

The welding robot above has a big generator and venting, and the cranebot below is spritely enough to climb high and lower a cable from his backpack.

The robot below has long arms that serve as a flatbed or dump truck and can scoop up lots of materials. The cement mixer to the right churns up concrete in his abdomen and then blorts it out his arm.

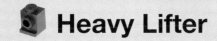 **Heavy Lifter**

56

This robot began as a construction worker flatbed truck. He is fun to pose because of the ball joints in his arms and the hinged clips that I used to make his fingers. Giving robots a personality brings them to life.

Two joints—one at the shoulder and one at the elbow—make him very posable. And his long arms make his poses exaggerated and funny, almost like a caricature.

"Who, me? What did I do?"

It turns out this guy is pretty good at flamenco dancing. You might say he's pretty light on his feet . . . but of course he hovers.

Beep Boop Bop

I love the look of retro 1950s science fiction, so I wanted this
rocket to appear like the future of the past. The red-yellow-blue
color palette gives it a classic feel.

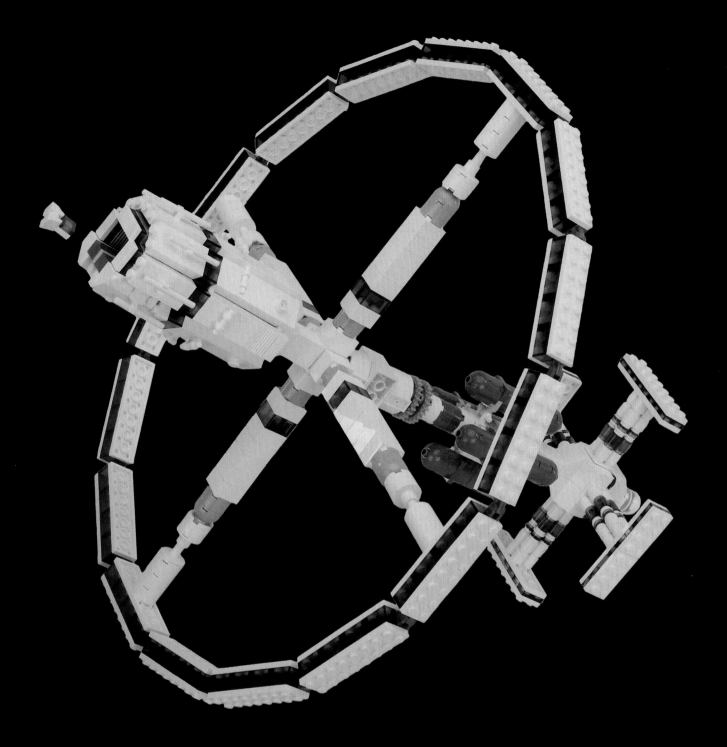

 **Space Station Symmetry**

The design of this space station happened organically—I started out building the very center connection using a brick that has studs facing out in every direction. From there, I kept adding more and more pieces outward, making sure it was symmetrical all around.

The design was inspired loosely by the shape of the space stations from the movie *2001: A Space Odyssey*, combined with the modular capsules of the real International Space Station.

A Plant in a Boot!

I adore Pixar's movies, and after seeing *WALL-E*, I was so taken by the film that I had to create a model for myself. It was important to me to capture the slight tilt to his eyes that gave him the cute expression of kindness and curiosity that defined him. I also spent a lot of time designing his arms. They ended up rather simple, but I created about ten different types before settling on the final design.

The "real" WALL-E does not have elbows, so his arms slide along an L-shaped track from back to front and then down to his belly. In my model, you can simulate this by attaching his arms to any of three studs on the sides of his body.

If you'd like to see how I built this model (and build it yourself), here are some breakaway visuals.

 # Pocket Bots

Most of these robots are only an inch tall, and each started out as a challenge to myself to use a weird piece in a crazy new way.

An upturned fender piece forms this robot's collar and chest.

A large cone eventually became the shell of this lethargic turtle robot.

Robot claws can clip to the round nubs on hinge plates. That gave me the idea for this robot.

Minifigure legs fit under a potbelly computer body.

This little guy's arms are axes, and his body is a wheel hub.

The fire hydrant is taking off!

Pith helmets for feet? Why not?

The slit in a wheel hub makes the perfect cycloptic eye.

This lady's cape is a Minifigure chair.

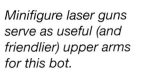

Minifigure laser guns serve as useful (and friendlier) upper arms for this bot.

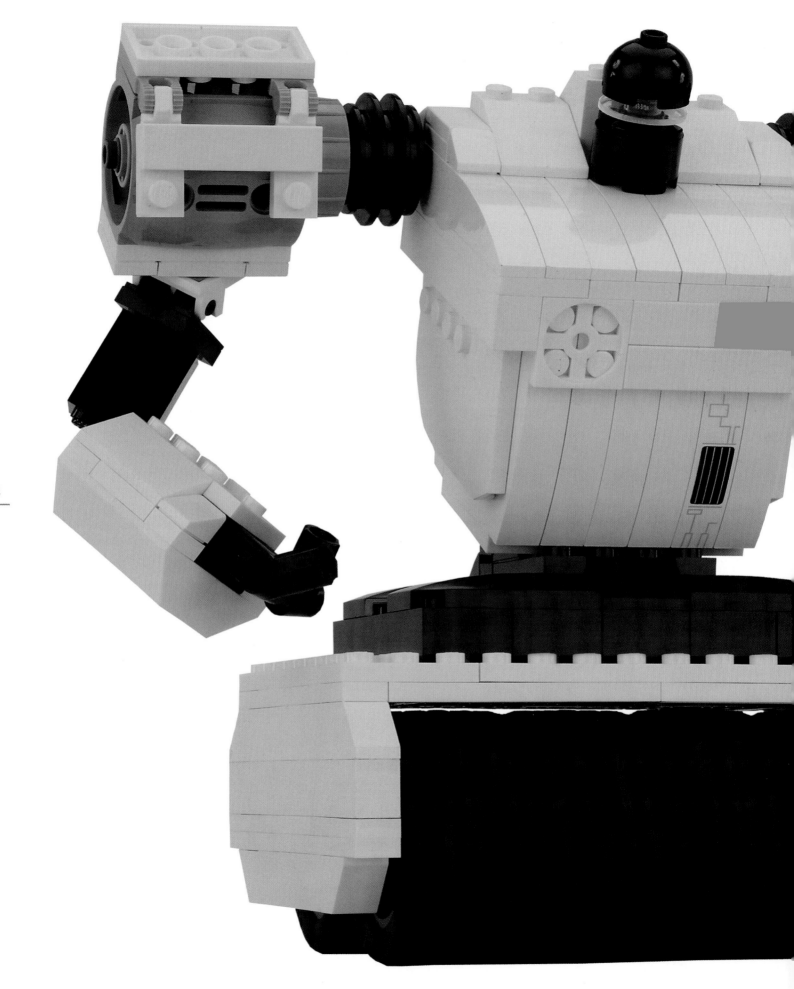

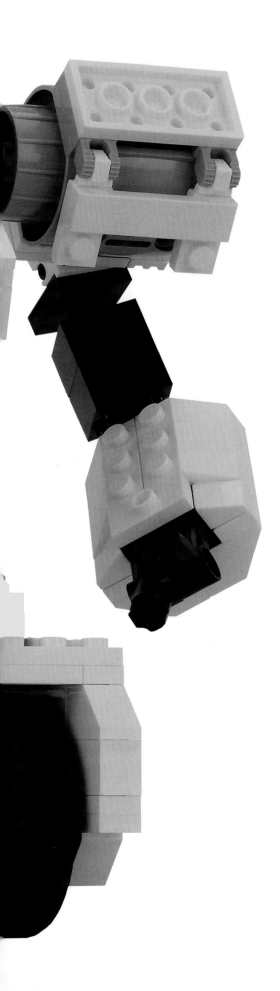

Not So Tough

I began work on my children's book *Cool Robots* in early 2008, storyboarding a tale of tough mecha, big cool battleships, lasers, robots, and spaceships in a world of neoclassic science fiction. I'd been building a litany of bots and dioramas of this nature for a while when *WALL-E* was released in theaters and changed my thinking. It wasn't until I found myself staring endlessly at blank sheets of paper that I realized I could no longer imagine a kid's world of robots and spaceships the same way. I literally went back to the drawing board and reinvented my robot book with a retro-modern *Jetsons* feel that was influenced by the world of *WALL-E*.

This robot was the first I created in that new style, and even though he's a big tough guy, he is barren of guns and rockets and violence. This style acted as a guide for the design of all the robots I later built and that are found in this chapter. As a parent, I look at toys and play in a renewed way, devoid of pain and conflict.

"I may look tough, but I'm just a big teddy bear."

65

 **Space Fleet**

I didn't know what these spaceships were going to look like before I built them, but I knew I wanted them to appear as if they belonged in a fleet. So I got all my red pieces together and began constructing them into whatever shapes they happened to become.

I created some rules for myself: each ship had to have white stripes, yellow blasters in the back, and a black cockpit. They soon looked like they all belonged in the same armada, swooshing off to the Swooshle Galaxy.

Wacky Bits

When building robots, I love taking unusual pieces and trying to integrate them into the design of the model. These three robots have Minifigure frying pans, wrenches, screwdrivers, and jackhammers as parts of their bodies.

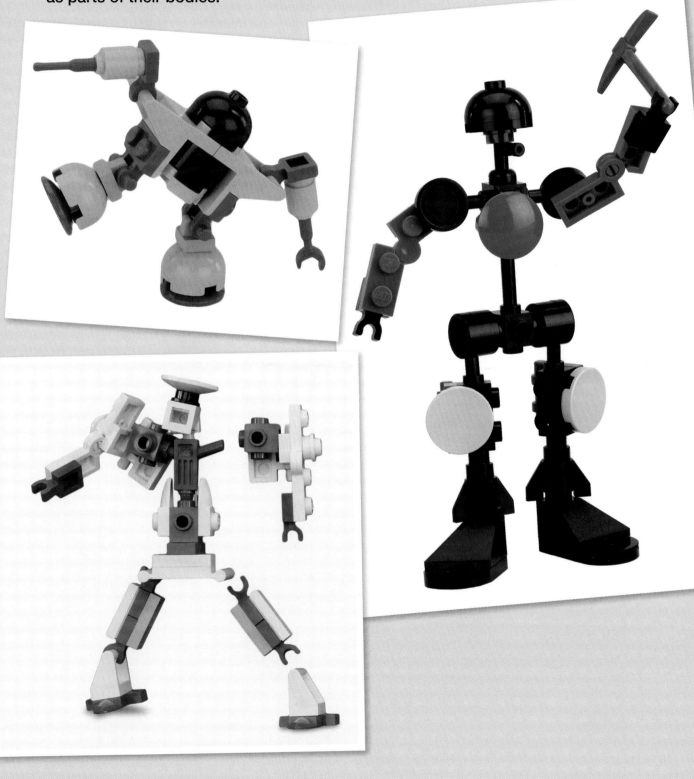

 # Gearguy

When I created this big Gearguy, I wanted him to have a retro 1950s look. He has lots of concentric circles, exposed gears and mechanisms, and a bit of a gangling stance.

Gearguy is built almost entirely with gray parts—only twelve yellow pieces and eleven blue ones give him his color. And did you notice? His fingers are Minifigure legs!

ARCHITECTURE

ARCHITECTURE

I live in New York City and love creating buildings, towns, and cities and adding all the life and excitement you find on vibrant community streets.

72

I took this photo from the roof of my building, located only six blocks away from the real Empire State Building. I built my model to look like it is lit up red, white, and blue, just like the real Empire State is lit up every night in different colors.

I'm inspired by cities everywhere, from New York to Copenhagen to Shanghai to Melbourne. It's fun to mix architectural styles from around the world.

The Ben Franklin Bridge

I built this model of the Benjamin Franklin Bridge live on a Philadelphia morning show in front of 6.2 million viewers.

I had to finish it in less than two hours, before the show ended! (The reporter even helped, and we finished just in time.)

I didn't make it to scale; it was more important to me that it capture the feel and characteristics of this local landmark.

The real bridge is located directly behind me and served as an awesome backdrop, but it also meant I couldn't make any mistakes because I wasn't fooling anyone!

🔲 Cool City!

This imaginary town square is inspired by lots of different places around the world. I wanted it to feel like it could either be the small part of a big city, or the big part of a small town. Many of my model towns don't have individual cars that contribute to traffic problems . . . just taxis, buses, bikes, and pedestrians.

I like to focus on the enjoyable activities there are to do in a city, like relaxing in the park or eating at a sidewalk café.

Roboplex Cinemas

Even robots like to relax in a nice air-conditioned movie theater. I'd first created this retro-inspired dad-and-son duo, and then decided to make an equally retro-inspired movie theater for them to patronize. The ticket window has been outfitted with an Automatic Ticket Machine Robot Vendor with Face (ATM-RVF) who spits tickets out after buttons are pushed on its forehead!

*Behold, Sir Buildsalot,
King of Confusingland!*

Old Architecture

Castles and cathedrals have some pretty amazing arches, wooden details, paintings, stained glass, and textiles. It was fun to create the gray-checkered tile floor in this castle—all the pieces lie sideways. And take a look at the two flat red tapestries in the back. Can you tell what I used for the yellow tassels at the bottom? (The short, stubby ends of click hinges!)

Once Upon a Time

Before building this medieval village, I had to do a lot of research on the building styles of the Middle Ages. Many of these buildings are built in the Tudor style, which used walls of straight and diagonal wooden beams and steep sloped roofs. Tables of cheese were optional but highly regarded.

Quack, quack! I was experimenting with white space while creating this scene of mallards and ducklings. Can you find the eggs that haven't hatched yet?

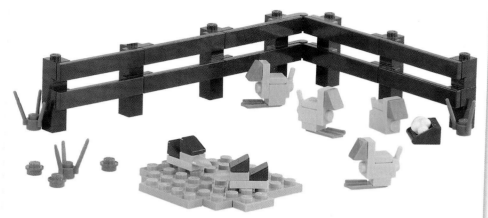

Chicago Tribune Tower

It was a joy to replicate this classic, Gothic-style skyscraper. Every inch of the building is covered in ornate details, making it a great challenge using nothing more than standard, off-the-shelf pieces.

The top of the building is covered in detailed facade work, made doubly complex by the octagonal shape and multiple setbacks. It's hard to make an octagon out of rectangular bricks—especially one that is covered with doohickies and greebles.

Did you notice the building's windows have shades behind them? Some are open, some are closed, and some are halfway in between. It takes a lot longer to construct the building this way, but it really adds life to the model when you later decide to go Godzilla on it.

City Walk-Ups

These early-1900s walk-ups all have the same basic plan; they're twelve studs wide and have cornices and stoops and a good amount of plastic "ironwork." But their similarities end there, as each has its own flavor and style. I make up stories for them all. The building with the yellow signs had an addition constructed on the roof that doesn't match the original architectural style.

The third brownstone from the left was converted to apartments but has no air-conditioning, hence the window units. The rightmost building was refaced with a low-budget modern exterior. The tall gray building was converted to offices by a real estate investor who also put a cell tower on the roof and two floors of retail at the street level.

Creating these stories helps me decide how each building will look and what characteristics it will have.

Building Buildings No One's Built

Every year I build models of real hotels for Marriott to give as gifts to their construction teams. The styles vary from low-budget interstate buildings to modern downtown high-rises and old commercial buildings that have been retrofitted into hotels.

Tulsa, Oklahoma

San Diego, California

San Antonio, Texas

Normally, when I create models of buildings I pore over whatever photos I can find, including online satellite and street views. But most of the hotels I build for Marriott are new constructions, so there are no photos to work from. I've had to learn how to read blueprints and architectural renderings to make the model accurate.

It's always fun to try to represent all the interesting architecture of the real buildings on a small scale, using the fewest pieces possible, given the amount of space available.

Arlington, Virginia

This curved-front and slightly triangular hotel was incredibly challenging to build. Getting angles to line up perfectly requires a lot of prototyping, editing, and rebuilding.

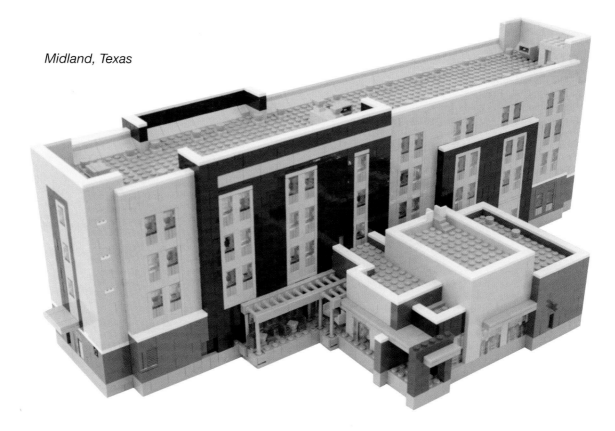

Midland, Texas

The models of the Marriott hotels are presented as excellence awards to their business partners.

Boston, Massachusetts

To bring buildings to life, I love to alternate white and black pieces behind the clear windows to make it look like the shades and curtains have been pulled by the miniature inhabitants of the building.

New York, New York

The New York Stock Exchange Building

The New York Stock Exchange asked me to build a three-foot-tall replica of their famous building on Wall Street. The completed sculpture contains over 14,500 pieces and is on display inside the real building.

The New York Stock Exchange is over a hundred years old. It was built in the neoclassical style, made to resemble old Greek and Roman architecture from thousands of years ago.

There are many tiny details in this model, which made it incredibly fun to build. The large columns are topped with ornate, leafy Corinthian capitals. Each capital contains nearly eighty small pieces!

Here's a close-up of the two-brick-tall lettering that I often use. Designing the K in this style was tricky. It isn't perfect, but it does the job.

The 1:20-scale figures are twenty times smaller than life size and are built with basic slopes, hinges, and rectangles.

White, white, white! The fun part of making something in just one color is that all the shapes blend together. These railings use cones, circles, dishes, slopes, and rectangles oriented sideways, upside down, and right-side up to simulate the swirly, ornate stonework found on the real building.

95

The fresco atop the columns contains nine larger-than-life figures, which took me three full days to build! It was fun to replicate the figures' dramatic poses with cartoon-like exaggeration.

I used to live just a few blocks away from Wall Street, so building this iconic old neighbor of mine was especially meaningful to me.

Times Square

I had always wanted to create a model of Times Square, but I was particularly inspired after the city closed Broadway to cars and turned Times Square into a new public plaza. The city planners painted the street tan to look like a sidewalk and set up chairs and road cones. Mere minutes after they did this, I sat down in a folding chair in the center of what had just been four lanes of Broadway traffic and simply enjoyed being in Times Square. I was proud to be a New Yorker and to live in a city that understood that streets are for human interaction as much as they are for getting from place to place.

With this model, I wanted to capture the bustle and excitement of the new public space, while still poking fun at the overall glitz of Times Square. Giant billboards, flashing lights and video screens, logos and signs . . . everything competes for your attention.

This model was on display at the Time Warner Center in Manhattan for four years.

New York's Broadway is all about theater, so I decided to create billboards of classic Broadway shows. How many do you recognize?

Until I built this model, I never realized how ornate the gray building below was. It has statuettes and beautiful detailing on every side. It has since been completely covered with twenty-story-tall television sets.

The Times Square model is wired with flashing marquee lights (made with strings of holiday lights), and the famous TV tower is fitted with digital picture frames. It is over five feet long and four feet tall, contains approximately 22,000 pieces, and took 300 hours to build.

🔧 Shiny Windows

These two buildings were made for a magazine cover and then photographed with professional child models. The buildings are hollow, but I don't like that to be obvious when looking through the windows, so I placed clear pieces in front of solid-colored ones, giving the windows some sheen and depth.

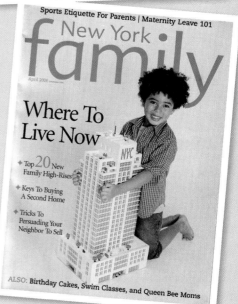

Empire State Building

This model of the Empire State Building is smaller yet much more detailed than the one on pages 72–73. In constructing this one, I wanted to push myself to create a better-looking model by adding extra detail and reproducing the shape of the building more accurately. I did a lot of research and visited the real building several times. After I was done, I decided to include a fun scene of microscale New York City traffic at the base of the building. (Which is lots of fun to play with—*vroom!*)

Little King Kong is up to his old tricks again!

This model now sits on top of the real Empire State Building, in the building's official gift shop.

The Eiffel Tower

The Eiffel Tower is an iconic visual landmark, and in creating this replica, I wanted to be true to the spirit of the original. I set out to illustrate the grand scale of the building by populating it with thousands of tiny tourists.

It was important to me that you could see straight through the latticework, the way you can in real life. There are no "cheat" supports to hold things up. . . . This miniature should feel as authentic as the real thing.

The model is used annually as the centerpiece to New York's largest Bastille Day celebration.

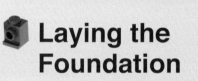

Laying the Foundation

Like real buildings, it takes a very long time to build the base of a large-scale model. I spent nearly half my time on this project working on just the first two floors of this building!

It's a long way down! This model of Chicago's Water Tower Place is over six feet tall!

The shape of this building is very simple—it's just a few rectangles—but the first two floors contain all the details from the real building: plants, banners, signs, revolving doors, a hotel, two department stores, a parking garage, a restaurant with outdoor seating, and lots of doors and windows. I researched lots of photos and street views online to make sure the building was accurate from every angle.

 Plastic Conservatory

When building scale models, I need only worry about what the outside looks like, but the giant glass greenhouse conservatory on the back of this building was an interesting challenge because I had to build a completely transparent structure and the interior, too! I wanted to make sure that the beams inside the greenhouse looked the same way that they do in real life, and ended up nearly replicating the actual architecture of the conservatory structure in order to do this.

Inside the greenhouse

House in the Hamptons

I was asked to create a model of a mansion in the Hamptons. It was presented to the owners as a gift and then placed on display inside the real house. My model is three feet wide, built with 5,900 pieces, and shows all the nice outdoor seating spots at the real-life mansion. My entire home is the size of the mansion's kitchen.

Old Stone House

The single defining feature of this historic center-hall colonial home in Pennsylvania is the fieldstone brick facade that gives the house a texture and a unique blended-color look. Initially, I assumed that replicating the stonework would be unrealistic, so I tried prototyping the house using a single color, but it just didn't look right in gray or tan or brown alone. So I decided to simulate the look of fieldstone with over 6,000 tiny 1x1 and 1x2

pieces in four different colors. Behind them, a row of big, blocky pieces gives the model its strength and shape. It took two weeks to build this twelve-inch house. Another feature I was particularly happy with was the little white cornice detailing. Can you tell what pieces I used to create the subtle white bumps below the roofline?

FAO Schwarz's "Bricktropolis"

I helped design and build an animated city that was installed in the world-famous New York toy store FAO Schwarz. Among eight-foot skyscrapers and a working subway train below the street, I created a lot of buildings and fun extras, like parking meters, streetlights, mailboxes, sewer openings, subway entrances, crosswalks, and other things you'd expect in a busy city, like a man walking his pet shark and three angry chefs running after a burglar with a pizza!

This tan apartment high-rise (left) is about three feet tall and loosely modeled after an apartment building on Sixth Avenue in New York City. There is a bank on the first floor and a motorized working helicopter on the roof.

Together with other builders, I helped create this display for New York's world-renowned toy store FAO Schwarz.

The Itty-Bitty City

The scale of this tiny city was designed around using a 1x2 plate as a car.

The buildings at the intersection in the foreground are micro versions of my Greenwich Village model (pages 128–131), and the rows of brownstones behind it were a nod to my studio neighborhood in Brooklyn. The waterfront promenade was inspired by a recent trip to Baltimore, Maryland.

Subway Cross Section

When I first moved to New York City, I was amazed by the design simplicity of the stations. I was also shocked to learn that a subway train is only about 50% wider than a taxi.

Mirrored-Glass Building

I knew that I wouldn't be able to use actual reflective glass or mirrors in the model, so I spent a lot of time prototyping and designing different ways of building the facade to simulate a mirrored effect. Mirrors fool your eye into thinking you are looking at something farther away. That, coupled with the fact that this building mostly reflects the sky, makes the real building melt away into the skyline without looking imposing.

To replicate this with regular pieces, I created the building several layers thick. The outermost layer is clear pieces; behind them are various shades of translucent blue, white, and smoky-colored pieces; and behind that are opaque sky-blue pieces.

Looking at the model, your eye is fooled by the depth of this semi-opaque facade, and you catch glimpses of reflection together with varied colors from the depth of the walls, duplicating the effect that you get looking at a mirrored-glass building: Your eyes don't quite know where to focus or what to look at.

A Health-Care Community

This neighborhood contains buildings that patients would encounter in any health-related situation: an insurance company high-rise, a hospital, a local doctor's office, a medical lab, a pharmacy, and a patient's home. I wanted each building to be immediately recognized as the "community member" that it represented.

This was easy for some of the buildings—like a single family home—but difficult for others. For example, what does a doctor's office look like? Some are at Main Street storefronts, others are in strip malls, and others are located in medical complexes.

I enjoyed coming up with designs for some of these more ambiguous buildings: The insurance company is a monolithic glass-and-steel high-rise from the late 1960s. The doctor's office was designed to look like it belonged in a relatively new suburban professional park. The pharmacy's design was inspired by the look of Walgreens locations, and I imagined the medical lab was located in an industrial park built with corrugated steel and a low-slung metal roof. Lastly, I made up a story for my imaginary hospital: It was originally built in the 1950s as a plain white tower on a low budget. In the 1970s, an ugly brick-and-concrete brutalist addition was tacked onto the side of the building. Later, in the late 1990s, a glass-and-steel atrium was added to join the two sections and to expand the first floor's emergency room.

Doctor's office

Patient's home

Playing with Scale

This model of New York's famous Chrysler Building is four feet tall and has a terrific secret. The building is built using what's called "forced perspective," causing it to look taller than it really is. The first floor of the building is constructed to the scale of a Minifigure, about seven bricks tall. But the next floor is only about five bricks tall, and the next is only four bricks tall. As you move up the building, the floors get shorter and shorter until they are finally each only one brick high! This gives the building the illusion of being much taller than it really is. If a model this size was built to Minifigure scale, it would normally only have nine or ten floors.

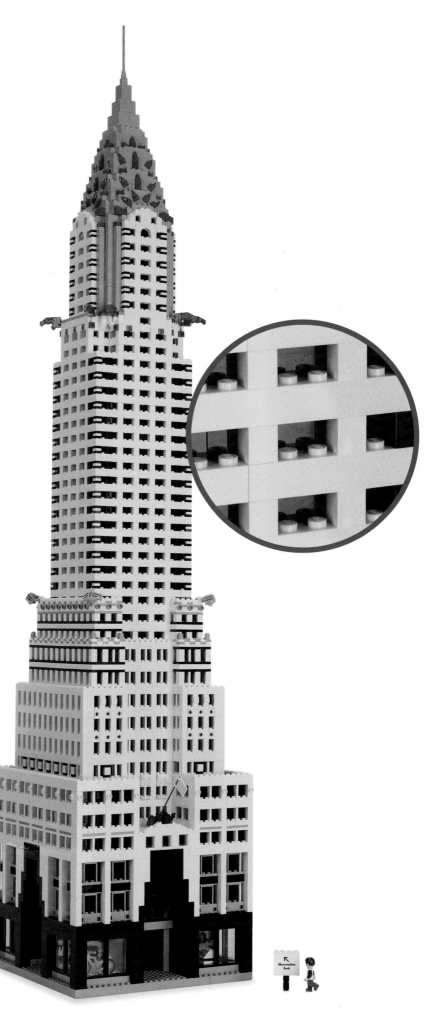

TownePlace Suites Hotel, Dallas

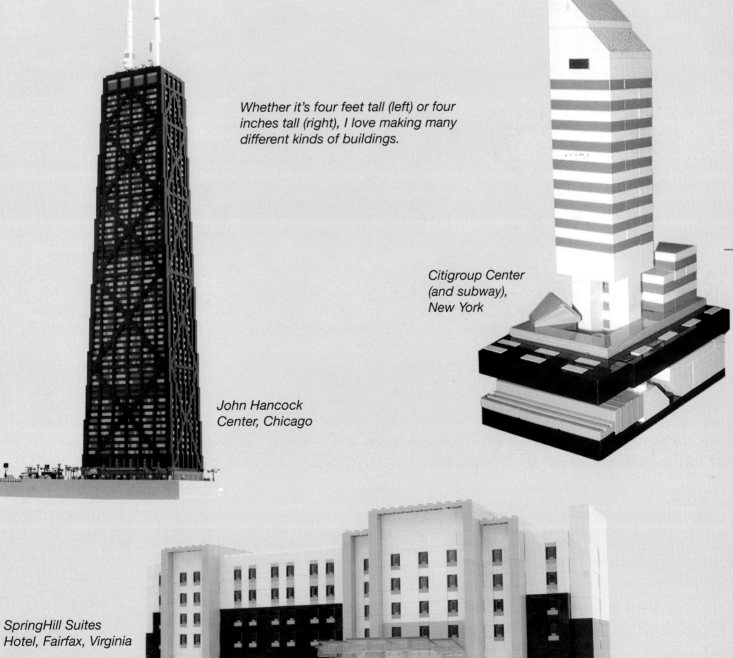

Whether it's four feet tall (left) or four inches tall (right), I love making many different kinds of buildings.

John Hancock Center, Chicago

Citigroup Center (and subway), New York

SpringHill Suites Hotel, Fairfax, Virginia

Data Center City

Commissioned by Microsoft, this diorama shows a hydroelectric-powered data center providing services to a town full of people in their homes, at offices and cafés, and in the park. A cross section of the data center shows how server systems, backup generators, and mega cooling systems are set up. . . . All were faithfully re-created from photos of real data centers.

A mix of architectural styles helps you guess the buildings' functions quickly: home, office, café, etc.

The diorama is sixteen square feet and was built with 28,321 pieces over the course of five weeks. My assistants Ji Yoon and Jung Ah helped design some of the buildings. The buildings are not replicas of real places, but they take their design cues from typical architectural styles of office buildings and single-family homes.

Real Architecture

Can you imagine having a bedroom this cool?! This one-of-a-kind built-in sleeping loft was constructed as a surprise gift for a young boy whose parents were renovating their Manhattan loft apartment.

This model was not predesigned—it was a spontaneous, free-form building process. The homeowners were very involved, providing their own direction as the sculpture grew: "More stretchy marks! But not blotchy . . . just clumpy!"

Constructing the staircase was a challenge. Building upward row by row around a wood-and-steel frame required us to think about how the color patterns and shapes would come together. This was made doubly hard because nearly none of the sculpture rests on the ground! We built ten feet up, making sure every piece was perfectly straight and aligned with the steel and wood beams. (Sure, no problem.)

Greenwich Village

Greenwich Village in New York City is a neighborhood where buildings are charming, not imposing.

128

Taking a page from Walt Disney World's Main Street USA (where buildings are built to seven-eighths scale), I constructed the upper floors of these buildings on a smaller scale to give the structures a quaintness, while still remaining realistic.

The model contains eighteen detailed buildings and scores of New York–style embellishments . . . tourists, taxicabs, parking lifts, bagel shops, authentic signage, and so on. The model doesn't attempt to replicate any particular place or any specific buildings. Rather, the goal was to imitate the feel of the atmosphere, the clutter, and the bustle of this bohemian part of the city.

PLANTS & INSECTS

PLANTS & INSECTS

🧱 Orchids

This life-size sculpture of a moth orchid is nearly three feet tall and contains 2,300 teeny-tiny pieces. All my sculptures are built with regular off-the-shelf pieces, and there is a very limited selection of pink on the market. I was forced to use only four different types of pink rectangular bricks to make this orchid look as realistic as possible, which made the sculpture even more complicated to build.

So basically this sculpture is thin, tall, jiggly, and built out of tiny pieces that don't have lots of connections and overlapping. More than once, I found myself crawling under the desk I build at, looking for a half-smashed petal or two.

I made three of these orchids, one for display in a high-end shopping mall in Hong Kong; the other two travel to botanical gardens and arboretums across North America. (I love to set them up next to real flowers and see if anyone notices the difference.)

Monarch Butterfly on a Milkweed

I was interested in showing the beauty in the symbiotic relationship between the monarch butterfly and its host plant, the milkweed flower. I posed them together, making both elements look weightless and delicate. The butterfly has an eight-foot wingspan, and the sculpture uses more than 60,000 pieces.

The sculpture is constructed around a central steel rod that keeps it bolted to the ground for protection from wind, weather, and theft. The rod also helps support the flower, giving the sculpture a weightlessness that belies its 250 pounds. And the antennae bobble in the breeze!

Such details made putting the sculpture together incredibly time-consuming (four months), but they also make it very beautiful.

Giant Terrifying Bee

This larger-than-life flying bee is over four feet long and has a six-foot wingspan! The sculpture contains 16,383 pieces and took four weeks to design, build, and glue. It is suspended fifteen feet in midair!

Putting on the finishing touches before the photo shoot.

Valerie and Natsuki build the wings.

Dragonfly

What's eight feet long, five feet tall, and really, really pink? Why, a 300-pound dragonfly, of course!

This sculpture is designed to be installed just above water level in a pond or lake, with the metal plate slightly submerged, so that the dragonfly looks like it's flying!

After creating a much smaller dragonfly, I wanted to make something magnificent in scale, color, form, and even in fragility.

By orienting the wings diagonally from "the grid" of pieces, it made it possible to add the texture of the wing's veins, which gives more character and a delicate touch to the sculpture.

The smaller four-foot dragonfly helped inform the design of the eight-foot sculpture.

The Rose

This rose is built the way a real rose is built, with each petal furled around the next, gathering into a tight bud in the center. The sculpture is seven feet tall—a lot taller than Jung Ah, who built it standing on a ladder!

On display at Reiman Gardens, Ames, Iowa

143

This Room Is Too Small

It seems ironic that building things with tiny pieces requires such a large room, but when we're putting the finishing touches on a show that's about to get packed up and shipped out, space can get very tight! This picture was taken in my New York City studio. Notice how all the tan chairs are stacked up on each other, and the tables are turned on end to make more space for the sculptures. After these sculptures shipped out, I moved to a new studio ten times bigger!

144

Don't Destroy the Rain Forest!

Several years ago, I made three dioramas that show how a healthy rain forest that is later destroyed by palm oil plantationists can be saved and replanted by conservationists. The "healthy" rain forest model has micro versions of Borneo wildlife, including birds, bats, elephants, monkeys, and more.

When I was creating these models, I thought I'd only need to build about ten trees and then use a few hundred bushes and plants along the rain forest floor . . . but I was way off! As testament to the lush density of real rain forests, I had to keep adding more trees, more plants, more bushes, more vines, more trees, more plants, more trees, more trees—it didn't look right until I had over fifty trees and thousands of plants in the tiny 15-by-30-inch diorama!

Here Come the Bad Guys!

We all hear stories of trees being cut down by loggers. But afterward, when the rain forest is cleared, the "bad guys" plant palm trees so they can harvest and sell palm oil for use in processed snacks and health and beauty products.

Compare this model to the model on the previous page, and you'll see that it's an earlier version. The trees in the back corner haven't been cut down yet, but the river is running dry and only a few animals remain.

150

*On display at the
Philadelphia Zoo*

Yay! Replanting!

A conservationist's job is to replant native species of plants and trees. If you compare this diorama to the one on pages 148–149, you'll see that many of the palm trees have been cut down, some small plants have begun to grow and bring shade back to the land, and animals are starting to return. The section in the back that had not been destroyed serves as a reminder that there's still a long way to go!

Jung Ah and Geoffrey are either hiding behind this giant pansy or eating it.

Pansy and Bee

Bees are such an important part of the ecosystem; many plants and animals would not survive if bees couldn't pollinate flowers. I wanted to show this important relationship with the pansy sculpture.

This was the first time I'd used purple pieces. They're very hard to find and are not available in many sizes and shapes. Combining lots of tiny pieces into larger chunks made much of the model building laborious—but it's the best way to achieve a stunning visual. Together with the pedestal, this sculpture measures nearly five feet tall.

Giddyap!

Praying Mantis

To keep this five-foot sculpture's skinny arms and legs from breaking, each one touches another (or bends back to touch the body) for extra reinforcement. Sneaky!

Lily

After building a seven-foot-tall rose (pages 142–143), we realized it was hard for most people to see inside and appreciate the beauty of the flower and the shape of its petals. We decided to lay this lily down so you could look into it and view how the petals and leaves are furled.

This flower is one of the most delicate large sculptures we've built, so it was important to design it in a way that the various leaves and petals could naturally fall onto one another for support. In the upper-right photo, notice how many of the leaves touch back to each other or firmly grab the steel base for strength.

We had to layer many small pink pieces together to create the massive center of the flower so it was rigid enough to hold up its weight.

Germinating Acorn

This is a sculpture of an acorn as it begins its life as an oak tree, with leaves and shoots unfurling and reaching for the sun. It's over five feet tall and was built with 15,581 pieces. Sculptures that are either very thin or very horizontal are difficult to build. Working around an internal steel frame is even harder. My assistant Geoffrey and I had to overcome all these tricky challenges to make this one appear weightless and delicate.

The Ant and the Shoe

Once upon a time, there was an ant and a shoe. When they met, the ant offered to carry the shoe to exciting new places in exchange for some cool shade. They became good friends and traveled the world together. But after a while, the shoe grew lazy and she began bossing the ant around, threatening to squish the ant if she did not obey. The ant was sad and didn't understand why her friend began taking advantage of her. So she just kept walking. . . .

This story has no ending and no moral. Some stories, like life, keep going, even when you don't have all the answers.

Tiger Swallowtail

This is the first of two giant butterfly sculptures I've built (see the other on pages 136–137). I wanted the wings to appear to lift the body off the ground so that the butterfly looked like it was taking flight.

The sculpture is built exactly the same way as the wicker picnic table on pages 234–235. The challenge here was to get the wings' coloring across a diagonal shape, so I drew the pattern of a real swallowtail's wings on graph paper and then stretched that pattern across the diagonal wall of pieces as I built.

 **Creepy!** This five-foot-tall corn spider hangs from the ceiling, designed to look like it's descending from its web. The sculpture has a custom-welded metal armature that connects with a hook at the top so it can be safely hung, and the legs opportunistically cross each other to reduce the chance that they would be too fragile and break. (I thought it would make a most intriguing hat, but instead it ate my brain.)

Real Plants

It took over a month to design and build this life-size bonsai. Many, many prototypes were created before we settled on the final shape and design of the leaves.

My workbench often looks like this: a bin holding thousands of sorted pieces, a few hand tools (just in case), some glue, and a pencil or marker for making notes as I build.

To accurately model the gentle bend of the Guzmania bromeliad's leaves, I decided to create this model entirely in plates instead of bricks. (It took three times as long to build it this way!) Dozens of overlapping, crisscrossing leaves give the plant its signature pokey-starburst shape.

I created this botanical mural for a high-end shopping mall in Hong Kong. The image continues across several panels, which gives it a fresh and interesting look.

VEHICLES

VEHICLES

I love creating all types of vehicles, from trucks and trains to bikes, balloons, and buses. Building BIG lets you add a lot of detail, while building SMALL lets you make models quickly and easily.

These little Smart cars are built to 1:20 scale, almost entirely with basic rectangular bricks. Can you spot where I turned the pieces sideways to get the curve of the gray "swoosh" just right?

Zoom Zoom

These cars were used as part of a contest in Mexico; we set one up at every dealership in the country and if you correctly guessed how many pieces were in the model, you won a real car! (Hint: It's more than seven.)

*In total, I built twenty-seven cars.
There were 2,488 pieces in each model.*

 ## Basic Blocks

Because I had to make so many copies of this giant car in only three weeks, I kept the construction simple—the design is relatively blocky and everything is built using basic bricks. We had 108 wheels to make for the twenty-seven cars (4 x 27) and found out by coincidence that each wheel contained exactly 108 pieces! Each copy of the car also had a custom license plate that I printed with the car's production number.

ZOOM-004
SeanKenney.com

Making Many More Mazdas

After we created all the red Mazdas (previous page), the president of Mazda Mexico loved it so much that he personally requested a model of a Mazda 2 built to the same scale. And because I didn't have to make twenty-seven of them, I was able to add a lot more detail. See, for example, the detailing in the alloy wheels (upper inset), the curvature of the bottom of the car, the depth of the front air dam, and the color detailing in the taillights.

This photo shows how a model comes together. After drawing the car on graph paper, I build two-dimensional cross sections (1). From that I interpolate the curves of the car, creating a three-dimensional prototype of half the car (2). Then I create a final glued copy (3) by copying the prototype.

1

Oh No! Who Will Fix the Traffic Jam?

You don't have a lot of space in a big city, and cars take up a lot of room. Plus they're noisy and dangerous. Traffic jams like this one can easily be avoided if you take apart your cars and use them to build bike lanes and streetcars (see inset). Your Minifigures will thank you for it!

 Ding Ding!

This big red streetcar is over six feet long and has all the details of the real San Diego Trolley, including the seams in the body panels, buttons for opening the doors, and all kinds of random gizmo train-move-makery.

It was fun to "write" all the lettering and "draw" the logo along the side of the train car. Creating details this small always requires turning pieces sideways and upside down on tiles.

I always build while wearing a suit (joke), but I took my tie off on this day.

Can you build a Minifigure-scale streetcar like the one below? Where do the wheels go? How do they get the floor so low? I went online to find photos of real streetcars and learned how they're put together so that I could build this model. You can, too!

Wide load! Coming through! Why commute to work when you can just drive your house there?

Cool Cars and Trucks

The semi cab above is the same design as the cab on this car carrier (below right), altered slightly for each truck's purpose. I was struggling a lot when I was trying to design this cab, and had gone through many prototypes that just weren't coming out right. To clear my mind, I stared out the window of my Manhattan apartment and spotted a perfect prototype. A bit of divine inspiration! I immediately built the model you see here, and it's one of my favorite truck models.

Whenever I'm at the airport, I love watching all the vehicles running around on the tarmac.

I had to research how real car carriers work before I could effectively build this model. It was also tricky to build various sizes of cars to properly fill the car carrier. It gave me an appreciation for how hard it must be to load a real carrier with cars!

Honda S2000 Convertible

This car is 1:20 scale, or "Miniland" scale. Building cars like this is always a fun challenge. Convertibles are especially tricky because you have to build twice as much (the interior and the exterior) and get it all to fit in a very tight space! The parts that hold the steering wheel in place come incredibly close to the headlights, and the brake pedal is tucked right behind the pieces that hold one of the wheels together.

But it's worth it when you finally get it right and can hold it in the palm of your hand! (Just don't drop it!)

Each of the tiny white taillights is the very top of an antenna, turned sideways and set into a headlight brick.

185

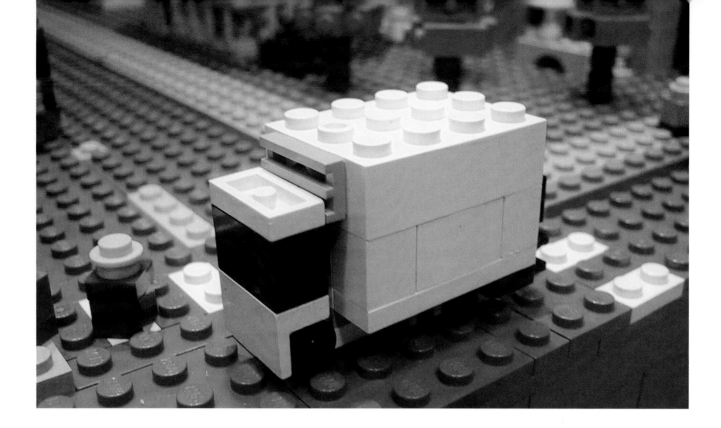

Microscale Trucks

You don't need a lot of pieces to build these vehicles. The tiny trucks are only three studs across, set in a city that's less than two feet wide. The refrigerated cube truck (above) has a gray grille piece for the reefer, and the cab is attached upside down so a thin wall piece for the front skirt can be used. The school bus (below) is frozen in time, midblink with one light lit up

on each side. (Although I couldn't fit a door. Oops!) Just look at how many more pieces you'd need to build a Minifigure-scale school bus!

Bike Share Triumphs Taxi

I was invited to contribute a piece to an art show that travels across Australia. The show organizer was collecting transportation-themed works from around the world and had asked me to contribute a piece that showed an iconic mode of transportation from New York City. I was first asked to build a classic yellow cab, but I am most excited about New York's new bike share program. Since bike share is the functional equivalent of taking a taxi, I opted to create a beautiful new bike triumphing over the old-fashioned clogged masses of taxi traffic. This piece serves as a bit of a visual pun on my own past work, staged identically to my piece *Bicycle Triumphs Traffic* (pages 306–307) because the message is the same: Riding a bike is a triumph over taking a taxi. It's cleaner, greener, healthier, faster, less expensive, and much more enjoyable.

Even though the overall message of this piece is conveyed by the basic staging and shape, it is still important to me to include all the little details, like the springs under the bike seat.

I used a lot of sneaky tricks to make this bike stay together. Where are the spokes? How is it standing up? Won't the pedals break off? How are the taxis fixed to the base?

A Nice Ride for a Very Big Kid

A lot of people tell me that I seem like a big kid. While it's fun to play with toys all day, I wanted to literally feel like a kid again, to feel small. So I surrounded myself with giant scaled-up versions of classic children's toys at my *Piece by Piece* art show in New York City. This tricycle sat alongside a giant rubber ducky, a huge xylophone, enormous fridge-magnet letters on the wall, and lots more.

*I tried riding this to work,
but the pedals stuck.
The tires are flat anyway.*

 ## All Abooooard!

This steam train was made with basic shapes in primary colors to look as much like a children's toy as possible. It's about two feet long and contains more than 2,500 pieces. Commissioned as a prop for an episode of the TV show *30 Rock*, the train was featured in a scene where Liz Lemon (Tina Fey) and Jack Donaghy (Alec Baldwin) needed to build it in a timed competition. I had to create eight copies as props, some of which could be broken apart over and over as they shot and reshot the scene.

 # Formula One

This four-foot-long giant car is actually just a scaled-up version of a Minifigure-scale car. I built giant pieces, six times larger than regular pieces, and then connected them together the way you would if you were building a regular-size model. The only cheat is the front wheels, which are attached diagonally on hinges.

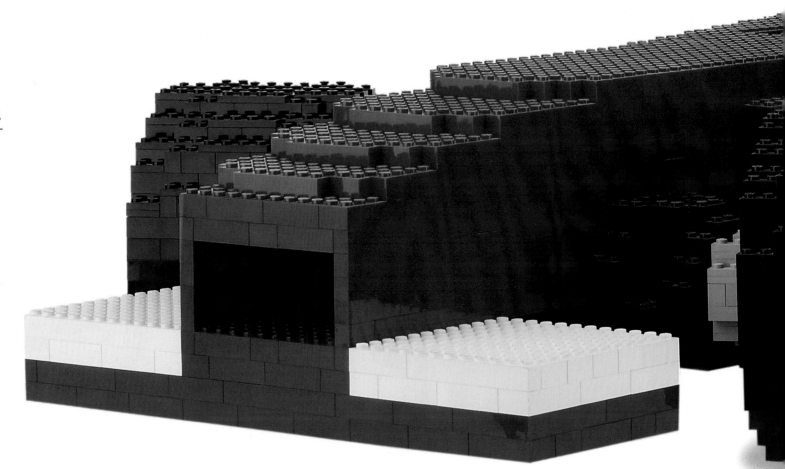

Ugly Vehicles Are Fun, Too

Panel vans are everywhere and have a million uses—construction companies, flower deliveries, TV crews, plumbers, phone repair teams, airport shuttles, dry cleaners, and ravioli deliveries. How many different types of vans can you make?

I wanted to put a ladder on the top of this van, but all the ladder pieces I could find were too long, so I built a ladder using two fence pieces and a long tile. It's the perfect size.

I drew the logo and the graffiti using a paint program on my computer. I printed them on regular paper, cut them out, and then used a glue stick to attach the paper to the side of the van.

I'm Full of Hot Air

I made this hot air balloon as a test before building a four-foot-tall version. I learned that this kind of model can't stand up because it's balanced on a teeny-tiny basket!

The clear and white pieces behind the basket help support this model. The four-foot version ended up with a metal stand inside.

 Bus

Building the iconic shape and colors of a VW Microbus is challenging at a small scale. My favorite detail is the ¼-stud offset handles, which I made by sliding 1x2 tiles just a few millimeters out from the side of the model.

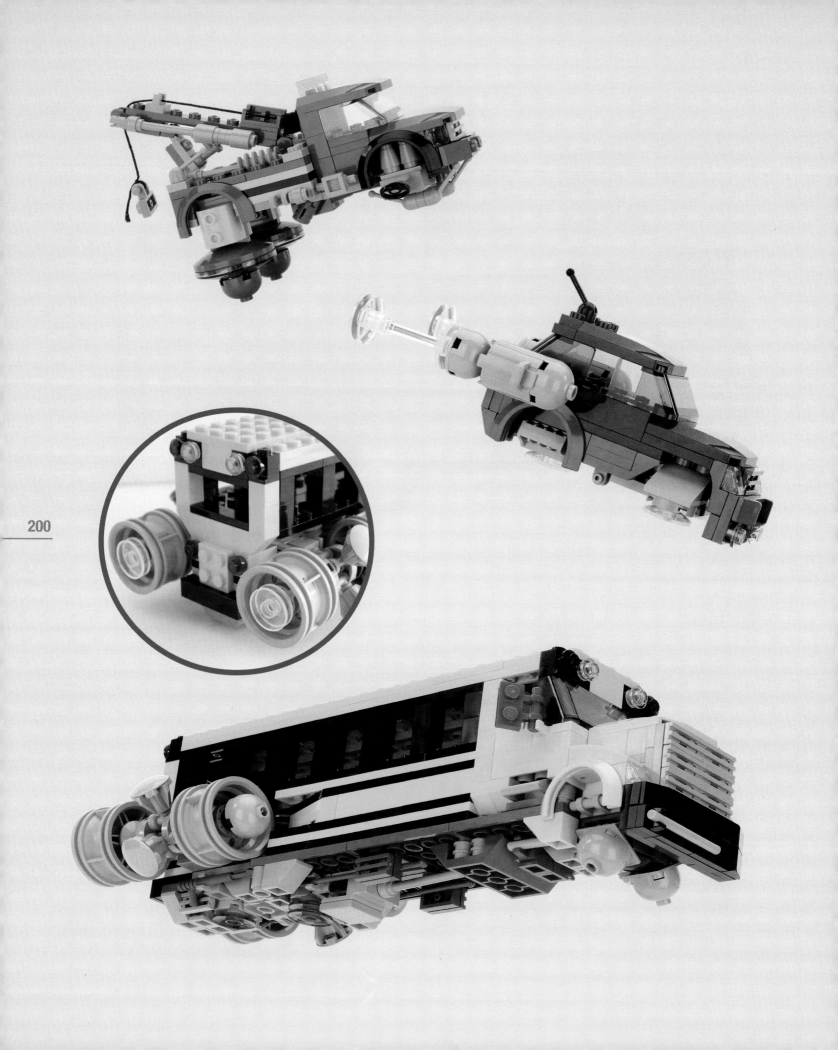

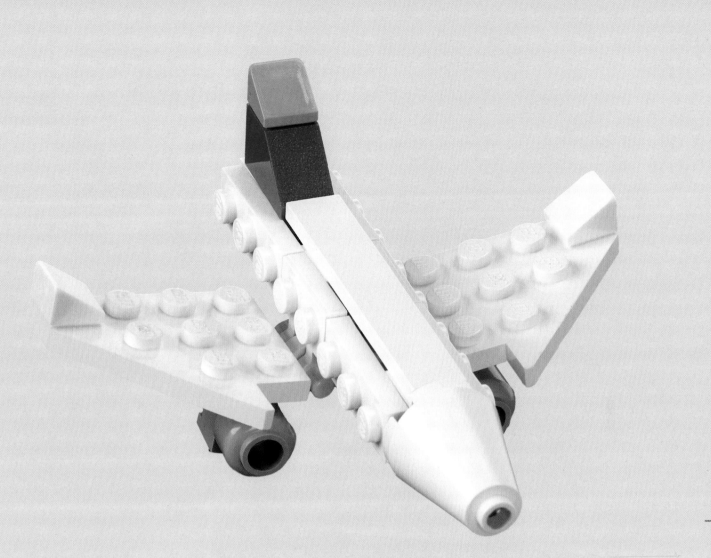

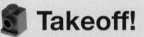 ## Takeoff!

You can turn any car (or truck or school bus) into a flying car just by taking off the wheels and adding hoverdooders. It doesn't matter what they look like (or that *hoverdooder* isn't really a word) as long as they appear cool and machine-like. The red vehicle has trash cans for its engines, and the school bus has wheels with the tires removed.

 **Big Flat Car**

This mural is ten feet wide and contains over 36,500 pieces. My favorite detail is the tiny orange highlight in the headlight.

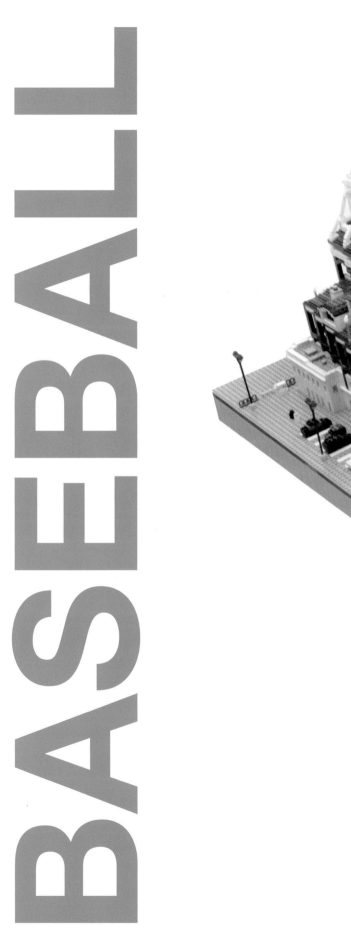

BASEBALL

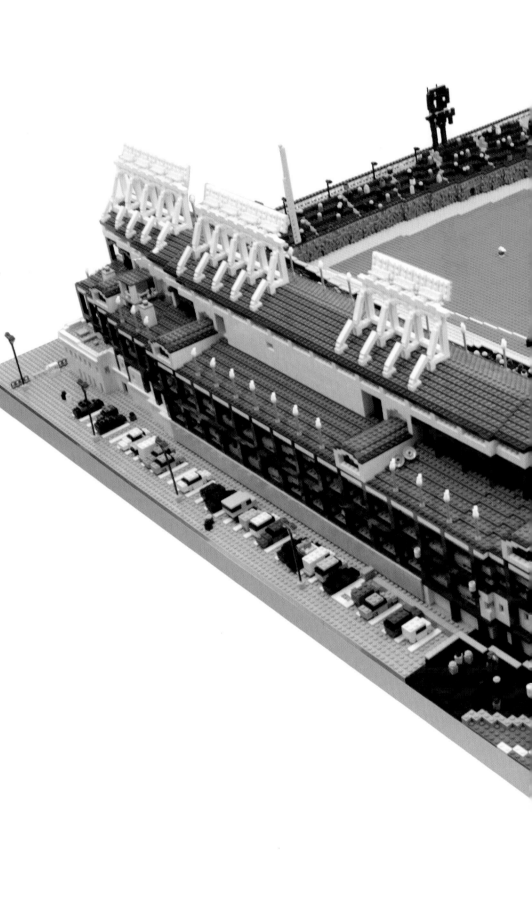

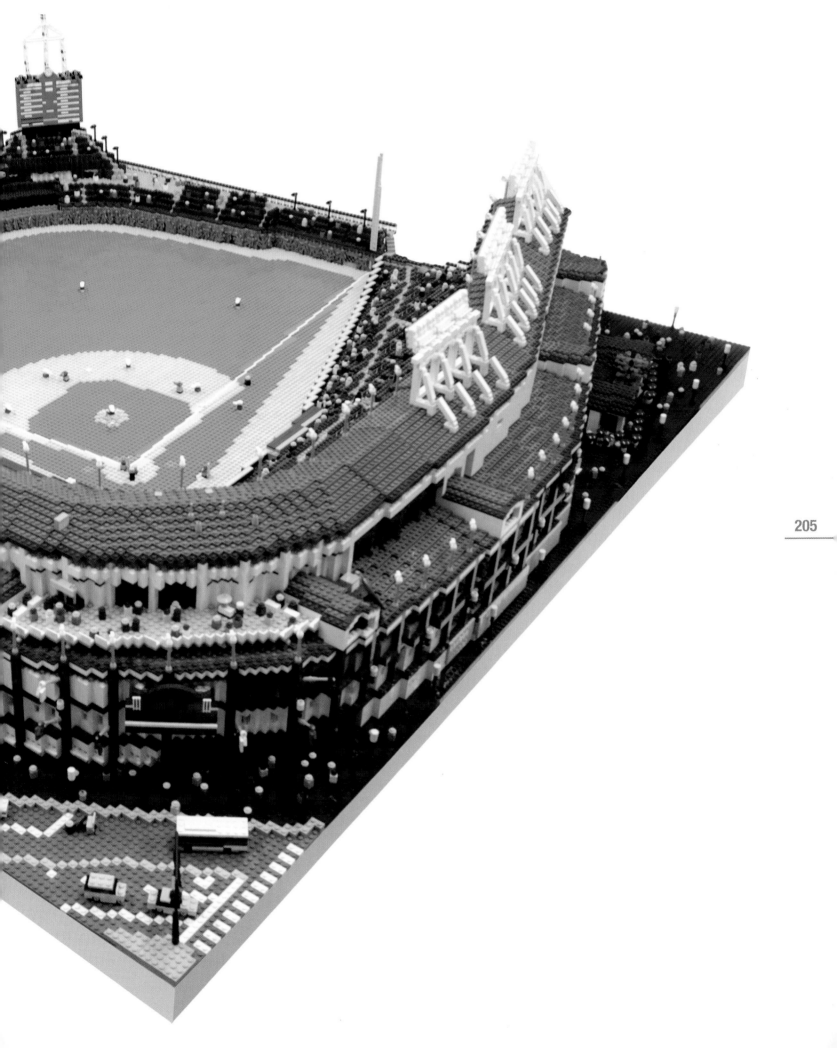

BASEBALL

Let's play ball! Baseball is a part of America. I grew up playing Little League and going to baseball games with my family, as so many other kids do. I wanted to create a series of baseball sculptures that celebrates what's special about baseball.

This series of figures, each in an iconic baseball pose, shows the moments of the game frozen in time. It's almost like the dance of the game; I wanted to focus on the players' bodies (and not facial details or clothing), so I intentionally left them featureless and monochromatic.

The classic Louisville Slugger bat, life size.

Black pieces don't read very well because they are so dark, so when you look at these figures in person, they almost look flat, like a shadow or silhouette. As you walk around them, the silhouettes change, and the figures look like they're really moving!

🔊 Take Me Out to the Ball Game

This mural of a baseball game in action is over ten feet wide and has a secret!
Looking straight on, you see a player at bat. But if you look at the mural from the
side, you can see clearly raised letters across the entire surface. They spell out
the full lyrics to "Take Me Out to the Ball Game," which has been a sing-along
at baseball stadiums for decades and is considered the unofficial anthem of
the game.

This mural was exhibited at the Louisville Slugger Museum in Kentucky.

Wrigley Field

Nowadays, baseball stadiums are architecturally uninteresting, glorifying corporate sponsors and commercial interests. If I was to create a stadium, it would be one that incorporates the history of baseball, something iconic and beautiful.

I selected Chicago's Wrigley Field, a stadium that has been a part of the sport for a hundred years. It's also an architecturally beautiful construction with its combination of brick, steel, and ivy, and the iconic red marquee over the main entrance.

This model is over twenty-five square feet, contains 57,960 pieces, and took 649 hours to build. (That's four months!)

Baseball stadiums are more than just buildings; they have an energy and excitement, and I wanted to capture that by including grandstands full of fans and the players actively running around the field. Other than the baseball diamond, there's rarely any one single large defining feature of a stadium. More often than not, a stadium is instead a collection of lots of little tiny details . . . fans, hot dog stands, speakers, lights, cameras, pathways and staircases, and more. The only way to really capture the essence and spirit of a stadium is to incorporate all these details in the model.

All the Little Details

This loading dock (above) might seem pretty dull compared to the
thrill of the game, but it's one of my favorite parts of this stadium.
I wanted to make it look like it was supported by white-painted I-beams,
which was tricky because the pieces I used are actually very fragile.
It was also challenging to make sure the other parts of the building lined up
properly around this interior space. Can you find my "signature"?

Microscale people are added in the stadium to bring it to life (above). America's favorite cartoon family, the Simpsons, even made an appearance! Can you spot them?

The exterior of the stadium (below) was a blast to build! I'm especially pleased with how the gray ramps look behind the green posts, and the shape of the grandstand lighting on the roof.

Out in Left Field

The real Wrigley Field has a big red Toyota logo here, but we thought it would be fun to make a pun out of it.

Why not have a snack at the restaurant (top) since the pitcher and batter seem to be frozen in time?

Sometimes the scale you're building at can work against you. Given the size of this scoreboard, there was no way to create the lettering and numbers with standard off-the-shelf pieces. But challenges force creative solutions like this one.

The outfield wall on the real stadium is covered in ivy, which I simulated with green leafy pieces, attached sideways by conveniently placed headlight bricks.

Big Leagues, Little Bricks

All my baseball sculptures began touring as part of an exhibit called *Big Leagues, Little Bricks*, which premiered in 2013 at the Louisville Slugger Museum in Kentucky. These sculptures have also visited lots of baseball stadiums around the United States and have traveled to Europe (even though most Europeans are not interested in American baseball!).

Mowing
Lawns

Chocolate

While exhibiting my baseball sculptures, I was asked to created portraits of famous contemporary players. So I created portraits of Derek Jeter, Joey Votto, and Buster Posey. A portrait has to be more than just what a face is shaped like—it has to capture a person's spirit. I was told these three players really enjoyed seeing their portraits, which is incredibly rewarding to hear as an artist.

HOUSEHOLD OBJECTS

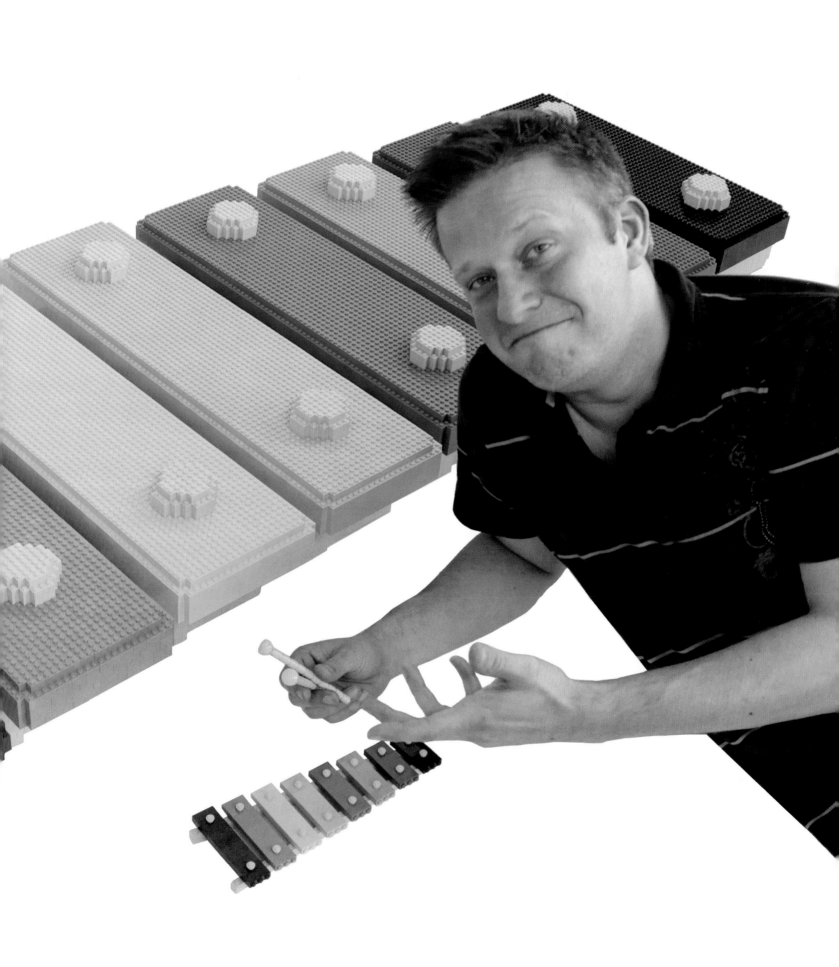

HOUSEHOLD OBJECTS

I like to build common, everyday things. This is a terrific way to make something come alive that might normally seem boring. (I mean, come on, a zipper?)

Scale doesn't always matter. You could take something tiny and build a larger-than-life version of it . . . or just the opposite—build a teeny-tiny model of something that's normally huge.

Zzzzip! This zipper can't actually move, but it sure looks like it can (which is the point)!

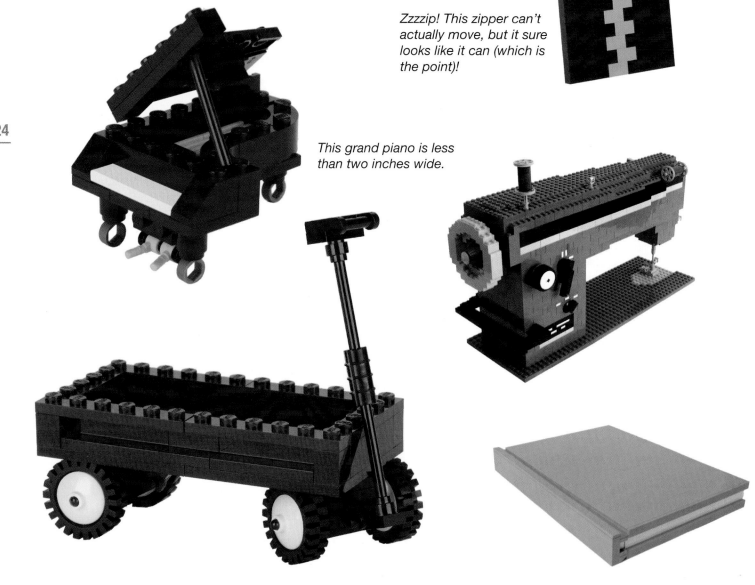

This grand piano is less than two inches wide.

I cheated a bit by using real tinsel on this Christmas tree, but it added a lot of flair, so I couldn't resist.

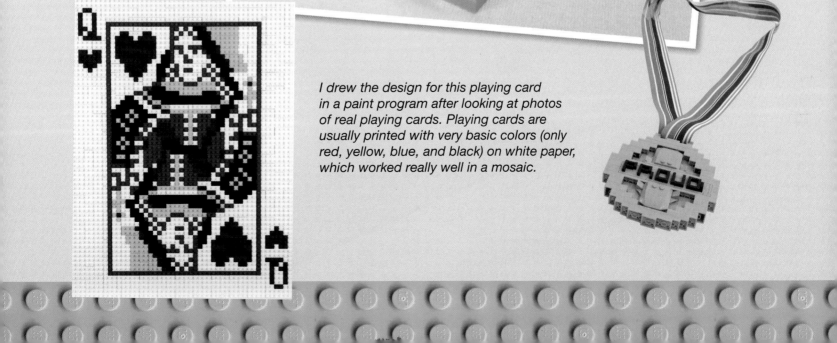

I drew the design for this playing card in a paint program after looking at photos of real playing cards. Playing cards are usually printed with very basic colors (only red, yellow, blue, and black) on white paper, which worked really well in a mosaic.

Not So Pocket-Size

I had only three weeks to create this giant 250-pound Nintendo DSi and have it installed at the Nintendo World Store at Rockefeller Center in New York City. I made sure to add all the teeny-tiny details, like the camera lens and microphone dot, the SD card door, all the buttons, and, of course, the two screens.

My favorite part of the model is the back, with all the lettering and screws.

I built a few life-size DSi models as well. Getting the proportions right can be a challenge, so I had a real one (above) that I used in order to get all my measurements correct.

 **Happy Birthday**

This was designed to look like a cake that looks like a giant 2x4 brick. (I must have baked it too long because it was very crunchy.)

The cake is incredibly large. The plate in the top photo is a full-size dinner plate, and the fork is nearly a foot long.

The candles are actually my favorite part. The flames are built with transparent neon-orange dragon wings, which came in an old castle set from the late 1990s. I only had two of them, so I couldn't add a third candle, even though the cake looks like it should have three candles.

Devoe, in green

Mercer, in lime (above) and dark gray (below)

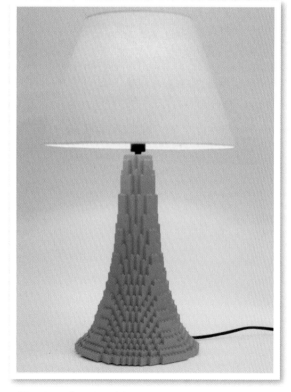

Stanton, in retro blue

A Real Working Lamp

Who says a sculpture can't be functional?
I love the look of classic-shaped lamps and
thought it would be interesting to make a series
of real working lamps. The bricky texture and
bright color is enough to turn a vintage style
into something new and different.

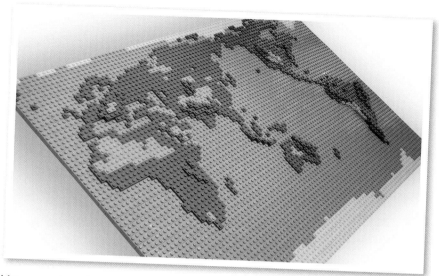

You are where?

E.U. are here.

There I am!

 # You Are Here

If you can create a flat mosaic of any picture, then why not create a map? And if you can create a map, why not create a relief map, with raised mountains?

🧱 Furniture, Big and Small

I prototyped this half-scale teak and wicker picnic table several times before arriving at the design you see here, which I felt best captured the curved lines of the table and the texture of wicker. To accomplish this, the entire table base is actually offset on a forty-five-degree angle, zigzagging the pieces diagonally to create a straight, textured wall.

The two chairs are about one-fourth the height of a real chair and designed to look like modern Danish outdoor furniture.

To contrast the texture of wicker, the teak tabletop was created by turning walls of bricks on their sides, to expose the smooth side of the pieces.

The red functional, life-size entry table is a modern take on traditional Chinese furniture design.

Sean Mower

While I don't have very fond memories of mowing lawns as a teenager, it's certainly fun to set this sculpture outside and see if anyone mistakes it for the real thing!

SEANDA brand gardening equipment (has been popular in markets that have never heard of HONDA brand gardening equipment!)

Push That Rototiller!

Machines are exciting to build because it's cool to make all the bolts and knobs and rivets. I used basic circles in lots of sizes to create all kinds of details along the faces of this tiller. And it really works! (Well, not really.)

PEOPLE

238

PEOPLE

Actor William Shatner (James Kirk of *Star Trek* fame) is amused by and defiant of the world of celebrities that he inhabits, after surviving typecasting that would have smothered a weaker personality.

The three miniatures on this page represent Shatner's past: the businessman in *The Twilight Zone*'s "Nightmare at 20,000 Feet," *Star Trek*'s iconic Captain James T. Kirk, and his spoken-word style of singing.

The miniatures are designed to sit in front of and beneath this ego-size giant bust of Shatner. The collection of models was unveiled as the centerpiece of *The Shatner Show* at an art gallery in Calgary, Canada. The pieces are now part of a private collection in Australia.

Miss Penn

This replica of the Pennsylvania Commonwealth Statue was commissioned by the city of Harrisburg and stands proudly at their visitors' center. Working from a miniature model of the statue and lots of photos, my assistant Jung Ah (right, inset) spent two months designing the sculpture. It took me and a team of four additional people 760 hours over the course of two months to build the steel-reinforced sculpture. The thin, wavy fabric, precarious dangling ribbons, and detailed face all added to the complexity. The sculpture is also too tall to fit inside a truck, so in order to get it to Harrisburg, we had to build it in three giant chunks (upper half, lower half, and a piece containing only her raised arm and staff), which were permanently put together on-site.

American Family

Parents magazine commissioned me to create an American family for an article they were running about family- and kid-friendly products. I was given creative freedom to make the family however I imagined them but only had a few days, so this was my take, inspired a little by my own family.

Wedding Cake Toppers

Among my most popular little creations are wedding cake toppers. I've made scores of them for people around the world, and customize them to match the bride and groom.

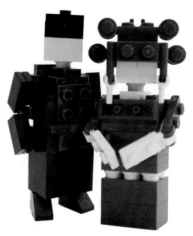

I've designed many hairstyles, beards, and goatees as well as grooms in kilts and military dress and have even added kids and babies and pets to the scene. Once, I created a Hong Kong couple in traditional Cantonese wedding attire. Then there was that time I was asked to have the groom playing hockey in a tuxedo that had his number on the shoulders. . . .

Do you, cat, take this dog to be your lawfully wedded beast?

Gardeners

This big guy in the green shirt (upper inset) wears a size-thirteen men's shoe and would be over seven feet tall if he was standing straight up. He's built almost entirely with regular rectangular pieces (except for a few round buttons on his shirt). I didn't want to give him a face because I wanted the sculpture to appear more like a mannequin so the focus is on his pose and what he is doing in the garden, rather than what he looks like. It was my attempt to capture man's connection with nature as he toils relentlessly in the garden.

I later added to this theme by creating a grandfather teaching his granddaughter how to garden (left).

247

He has absolutely no sense of humor.

🧱 I Certainly Have a Big Head

This self-portrait mosaic is probably my most egotistical creation, but I suppose every artist has to do a self-portrait at some point in their career. I wanted to use only the primary colors red, yellow, and blue (plus black and white) to make a very stylized, bold, and punchy mosaic.

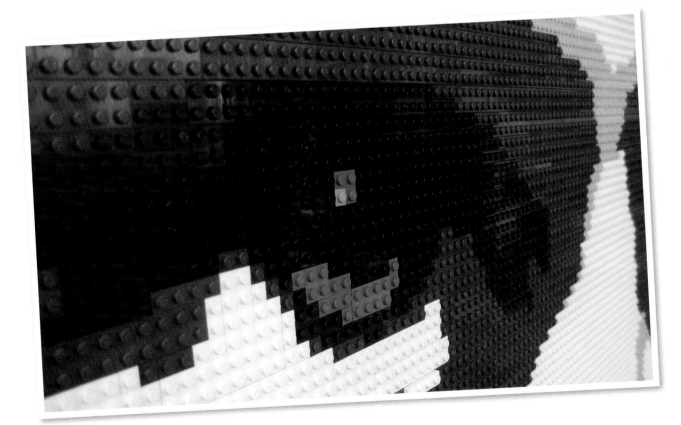

Gorton's Fisherman

Early in my career, I was commissioned to build the Gorton's Fisherman, of frozen fish stick fame. This was one of the first sculptural human figures I'd ever created and is still one of my favorites. I created nine copies that visited over one hundred supermarkets around the United States.

This sculpture is smaller than life-size, so it relies heavily on a piece called the "jumper" or "1x2 plate with single stud." The jumper lets you offset a piece halfway, doubling the detail level that is possible. It's critically important on models of this size that demand a lot of detail and facial recognition.

The sculpture is built entirely in standard studs-up fashion, except one section where I use a "studs not on top" (SNOT) building technique. So where's the SNOT? On his nose. Seriously.

Did you notice? The head is rotated about thirty degrees from the body.

Life-Size Busts

When I build a human head, one of the first things I do is draw the face on graph paper from the front and from the side. For a prototype, I build a cross section of both of these angles to get the proportions correct and then begin filling in the curves manually from photos by eyeballing it with lots of trial and error.

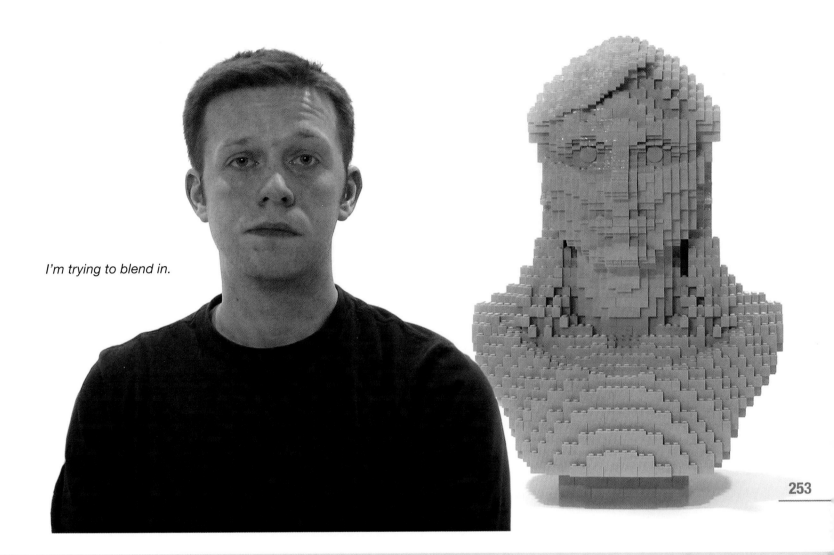

I'm trying to blend in.

I end up drawing all over the prototype, taping pieces on, and propping things up on scaffolding before I am happy with the result. Then I start all over again. . . . I build a second copy of the head—this time with glue so that it's permanent—using the prototype as my design model.

I created these busts for Herman Miller's award-winning design magazine, *SEE*.

I was surprised to find that creating monochromatic figures was more challenging than multicolored ones. Human features are very subtle, and without color changes to indicate where areas like eyes, lips, or hair begin and end, I was forced to exaggerate facial features and use depth changes and hard lines to define these areas. Too much exaggeration would be cartoonish, but not enough would leave the busts featureless.

I also wanted to make sure each figure had its own unique facial feature, hairdo, and attire. I modeled the yellow figure to have a large bone structure. The tan figure has a much smaller bone structure, higher cheekbones, and a pointier nose and chin. The red figure has a wider, more rounded jawline and a shorter nose. Every feature, from their earlobes to the shapes of their eyes, is different.

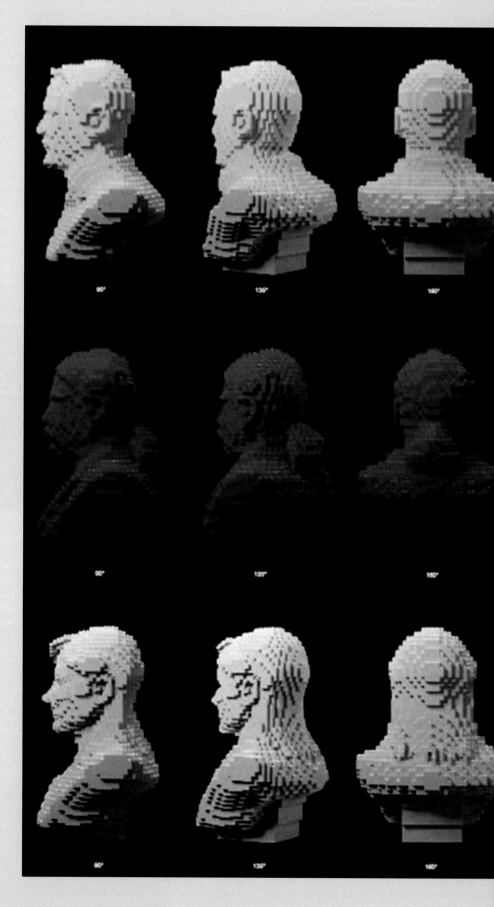

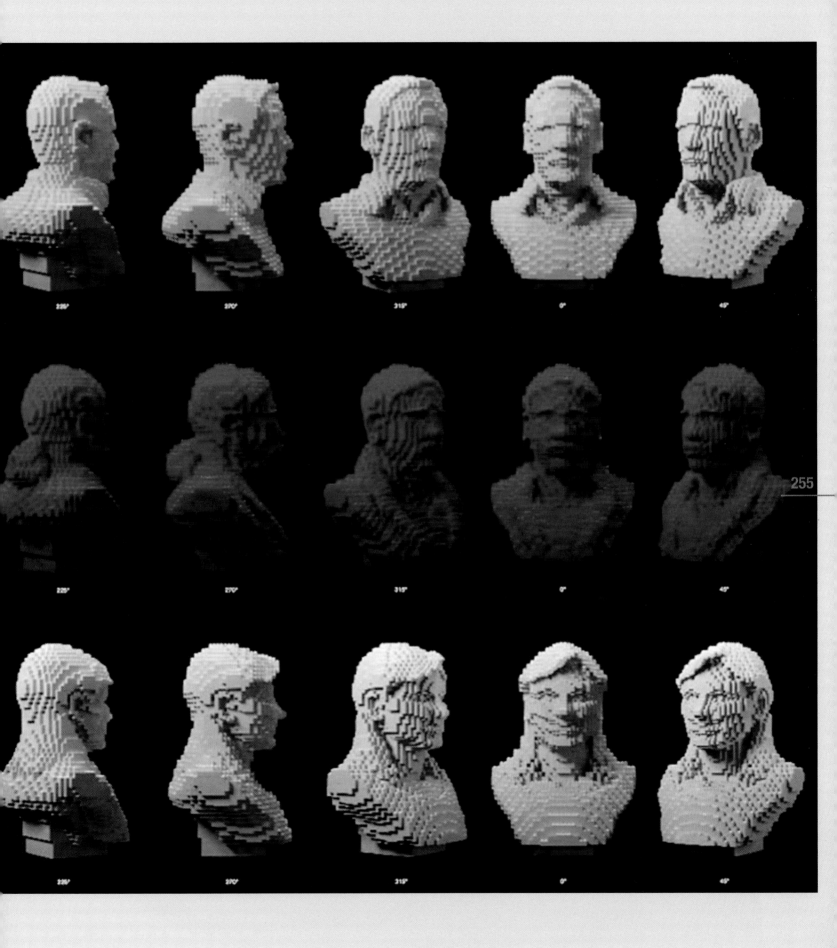

Making Real People

Imagine unwrapping a birthday present and seeing a big blocky mirror image of yourself staring right back out at you. That's what happened to these two brothers! Their mother asked me to design life-size sculptures of them as surprise gifts. Burk (right) ended up in a classic Greco-Roman shirtless style while his brother Zach (left) got a more modern treatment.

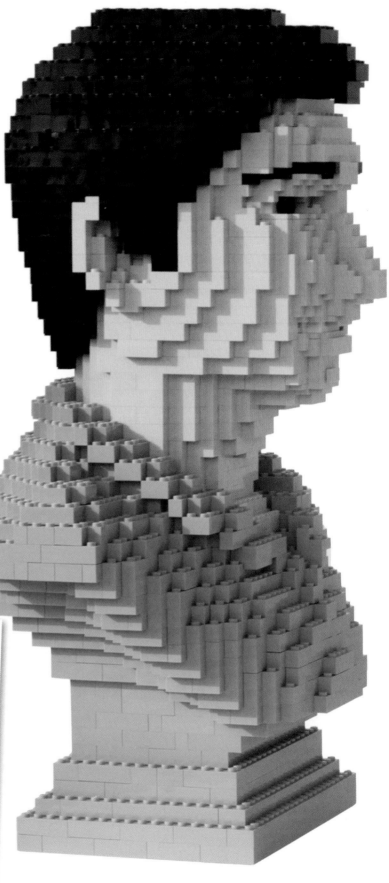

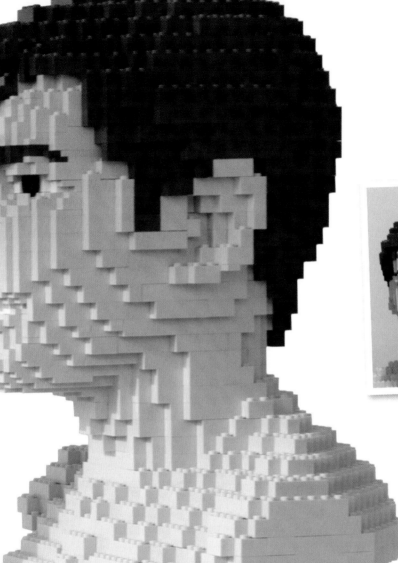

The classic look of Burk's sculpture bust has made it one of my favorites. I built a copy for myself and take it to events to show people how I create some of my sculptures.

Funny Portraits

I do a lot of portraiture, and I really enjoy when the subject has a good sense of humor. If you're all dressed in white on a white background, it's hard not to be a bunch of floating heads. Your stuffed monkey should have bananas in the background. And I have no idea what was going on in that Taiwanese wedding picture, but I love it.

"Vintage" portrait based on a photo taken in the 1960s.

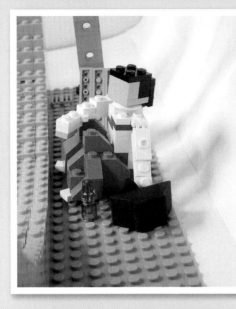

🧱 Skater Park

For many years, I was enamored with the 1:20-scale style of building, where you create models exactly twenty times smaller than real life. (Take a look at all the 1:20 cars in the Vehicles chapter!)

When I was younger, my brothers were both avid skateboarders. I was inspired to make this scene when I found myself with a surplus of tan plates and had the idea to build a half-pipe of skaters doing awesome tricks. The rest fell into place as I started creating these guys in a few dynamic poses. As a nod to my brothers, the guy sitting down is wearing overly baggy pants, which my brothers were fond of in high school.

(And of course the grandstand lighting always has a few bulbs blown out.)

My assistant David and I pose for a photo.

Say Cheese!

These things are such an old form of entertainment; people have been making them for over a hundred years, and yet, oddly, they have no name. Many people call them "photo ops" or "face cutouts," but I just call them a lot of fun.

To create this mural, I used my cartoonist background and drew a lot of cartoons with paper and pencil until I had this particular design that I liked best. I then scanned it into my computer and painted in all the colors in a paint program. The last step was to redraw a copy of the cartoon on-screen pixel-by-pixel to create a blueprint that we could print out and build from.

Planting a tree isn't often the most dynamic visual, but I wanted it to look interesting, so I included butterflies, insects, and flowers to add color and energy to the piece. The little blobby tree leaves are my favorite detail; they look so cute and feel like they're made of dough.

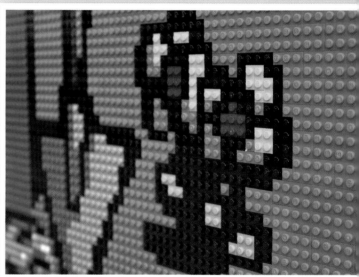

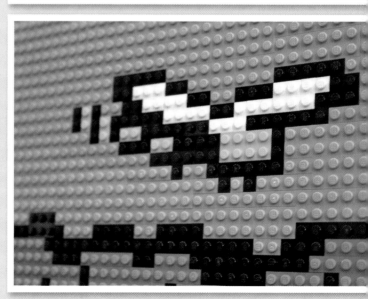

Two Short Orders

At diners, delis, and cafés, a short-order cook makes quick dishes like eggs and pancakes. In the stock market, big-time investors can place a "short order" to make money on falling stock prices, reaping huge profits off everyone's losses.

On September 15, 2008, a financial crisis erupted that shot ripples through our economy—major banks were folding, big companies were going bankrupt, people's retirement savings were wiped out, the governments of the world were panicking. No one was sure how or when it would end.

The next day, I was getting breakfast at my local deli and saw *Euro & Peso accepted too* written on the cook's tip cup. I realized that even though the short-order cook and the short-order investor were both in the same financial mess as the rest of us, at least for that one day, the hardworking person was the one making the money.

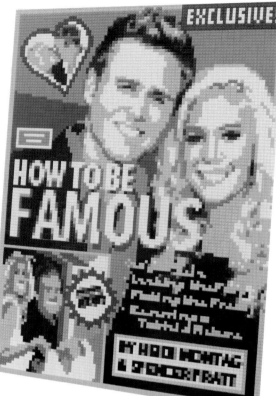

Heidi Montag and Spencer Pratt

Nate Berkus

Heather Anne Campbell

Famous People

I'm lucky to have been able to create mosaic portraits of a lot of famous actors, professional athletes, and television personalities over the years. Some of the portraits on these pages were commissioned by a show producer or a publicity team and presented to the celebrity as a surprise on live TV or as a gift. It's incredibly flattering for a famous personality to commission my work. Among those, Tina Fey, Drew Carey, and Zach Braff have each personally asked me to create portraits of their friends and loved ones. And Alec Baldwin once joked with me that he wanted to do a formal portrait sitting in my studio. (Although he never took me up on the offer, darn it.)

Regis Philbin

Kelly Ripa

Bart Scott

Derek Jeter

Buster Posey

Joey Votto

Anthony Anderson

Melissa Joan Hart

*Peter Norton and
Gwen Adams Norton*

🔲 Success Story

It seems that society puts very little emphasis on exploring one's creative side. We are taught that good students excel in serious subjects like math, science, history, economics, and engineering. We are taught that to be "successful," we must get good grades in serious subjects, and after college we will be rewarded with a good job.

So I followed society's advice. I got a college degree in computer science. I took a lot of math classes. I interned for three years at a telecommunications company. I was "doing the right thing."

But I loved art. In college, I cofounded a university art club and drew daily cartoon strips for a newspaper read by 40,000 people a day. Squeezed between my "real" classes, I enrolled in sculpture, photography, drawing, animation, and music. It never occurred to me that I got As in only those art classes. They didn't feel like work, because they came easily to me and I enjoyed them so much.

Ten years later when I made this model, I had a successful career consulting at Internet start-up companies. My job was to sit at a computer in a beige cubicle and write computer programs. I was paid well. I was respected. My environs were temperate.

I was the man in this model. Society told me I was successful. But I felt numb and uninspired.

So I broke free from
my corporate shackles
and dreamed to live the
unpredictable life of an artist!
I grabbed a million colorful bricks
and began to build whatever I wanted.
To me, there is no greater joy than to
be able to create something
with your hands that evokes
a response in others, from a
smile or a laugh to thoughtful
introspection.

Sometimes you have to follow your
dreams and trust yourself, even in the face
of those who may tell you otherwise. I firmly
believe that if you do what you truly love, your
passion will inform your work and you will
be successful.

🔲 Minifigures

Of course the easiest way to add people to your creations is to use Minifigures. Whenever I'm making a Minifigure-scale model, I enjoy adding fun vignettes to offer lots to look at as you explore the piece.

I snuck this (above) into my third book, *Cool City*, when my wife and I were expecting our first child. This is a little version of my wife pushing our baby in a modern infant stroller. (Years later, my daughter repeatedly asked why she only got to be a round 1x1 plate.)

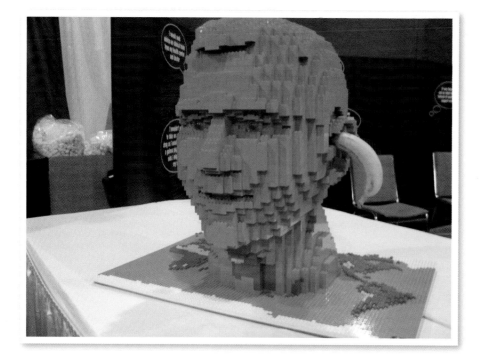

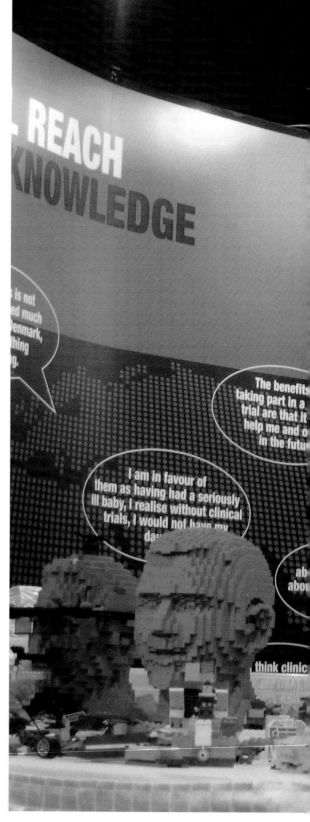

 ## Mr. Continental

What would it look like if a giant head stretched itself out of the earth? And could I build it in three days while a crowd of people talked to me and asked questions? I'm never one to say no to a challenge.

In order to create this sculpture so quickly, I prebuilt the eyes, the mouth, and the map base, and then built the entire sculpture "double up," with a 2x2x2 brick representing a 1x1x1 brick in a smaller prototype. That also meant I could build the entire model with only 2x4 bricks!

The Accomplished Man

At one point early in my artistic career, I started questioning why I was doing what I was doing, and what my motivation was. I felt like every time I accomplished something great, I'd look around and realize I was surrounded by people even more successful. It made my accomplishments feel anticlimactic. To this day, I still don't feel like "I've made it" because I'm constantly on a journey of sharpening my skills, trying new things, and most important—being inspired by the great things that everyone else creates.

Looking around at everyone else can be a lot like looking in a mirror, if you think about it.

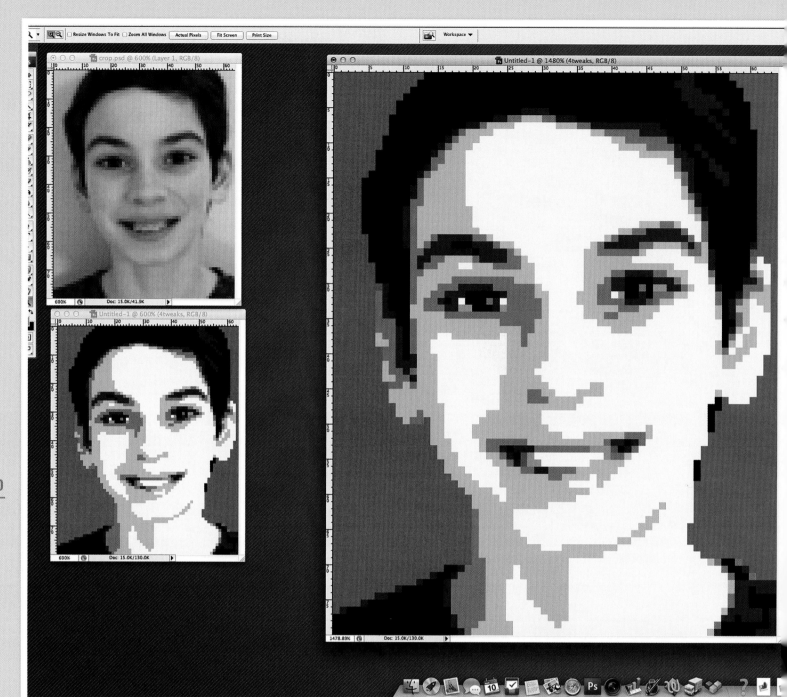

Making Faces

Many people think my portraits must be computer-generated. Nothing could be further from the truth: They are all hand-drawn illustrations. A portrait is more than simply what someone's nose is shaped like.

It has to capture the essence of the subject: It has to have a spark, a spirit, some kind of life. My portraits are always based off a photo (or photos) sent by my clients. I start with the original photos and begin drawing a pixelized version over them, like using digital tracing paper.

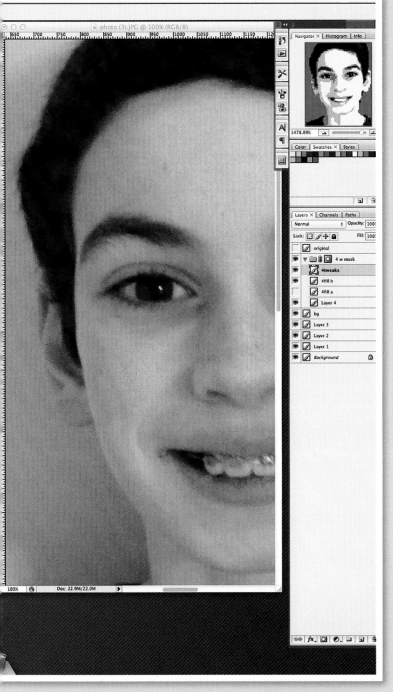

My drawing process

I create backgrounds that mirror the subject's personality . . . wild, calm, organized, absurd, or sometimes simply their favorite colors. I often make several versions and send them to my client for their feedback.

Hand-drawn

Computer-generated

The vibrant splashy background behind this couple was inspired by the distinguished-looking crow's-feet on this stately gentleman combined with his wife's colorful jewelry.

Sometimes when adding a background, I try to incorporate colors from the subject's clothing. This fellow looked like he had a good sense of humor, so I made the background a little quirky.

It's difficult to squeeze a lot of people into the same-size "canvas" because the picture becomes much blockier. The results, shown here, are often a bit cartoony, but I offset this by using only two shades of red (with black as a shadow) to create a more sophisticated color palette.

I love creating portraits of subjects together, because it really can show the love that people share.

Grayscale portraits are tricky because you have only four colors to work with.

Working with color can be hard; light skin tones can blur into the browns and blonds of hair, which can blur into gold and tan clothing. I do my best to make these areas appear discrete.

This pop-art "burst" background has become one of my signatures. I love it because it adds a lot of energy to a portrait. Typically I make these bursts two-tone, but for this one I used three colors.

To honor the passing of this young boy, I made the background "burst" emanate from above to look like the sun rays that form in the sky from parting clouds.

Drawing this decorated hero's myriad of medals took a lot of time. Here, white accents gray to imply chrome, and yellow accents orange to imply brass.

This boy's favorite color is orange. I used red as a "shadow" for orange to prevent his shirt from blending into the background. The left side of the background is orange on yellow, while the right side is yellow on orange, to simulate light falling across the background the same way it falls across his face.

EVENTS & EXHIBITIONS

EVENTS & EXHIBITIONS

My *Nature Connects* exhibition has been touring North America since 2011. My team and I built over 125 larger-than-life sculptures with 2.5 million pieces in total. These sculptures seek to illustrate man's connection with nature, the beauty of nature, and the various connections found within nature. Just as every piece in my sculptures is connected, everything in nature is interconnected. Insects and plants have important relationships. Animals have relationships with other types of animals and plants. Animals have connections with their families just like we do. And, of course, people have a connection with nature. Whether you're trimming a rosebush, planting a garden, or eating a meal, you are a part of nature.

Created in partnership with a public university, *Nature Connects* is foremost an educational platform and secondarily a means of artistic expression. I hope that you can look at *Nature Connects* and appreciate both nature and the sculptures as something beautiful.

On Their Way

Once these giant sculptures are built, getting them out the door of my studio is still quite a feat! It's always a treat for the neighbors when the art handlers show up to move the sculptures out of my building.

Even the New York Police Department stops to watch!

Next the sculptures are off to a crating facility, where they're put into custom-built museum-quality traveling-exhibition crates so they can be safely taken to and displayed at botanical gardens and arboretums.

Moving the Show

The entire *Nature Connects* exhibit fills five full-size tractor trailers! Each crate weighs hundreds of pounds and must be unloaded from the truck with a forklift.

My team of installers carefully opens every crate and inspects the sculpture to make sure it arrived all in one piece. The crates are custom-made with special foam-fitted interiors that keep the sculpture steady and protect fragile areas. Because of this attention to packing, it's rare that anything ever breaks in transit.

Steady . . . Steady . . .

The sculptures themselves are not always heavy, but each is steel-reinforced and mounted to a heavy steel base, so it takes a lot of us to lift and position them. Then the sculptures are bolted into place on-site to withstand extreme weather and overly curious fingers.

295

Not Really Floating

These giant Victoria water platters and koi fish look like they're really floating in the pond—except they actually weigh hundreds of pounds and would sink in a moment! To accomplish this illusion, I designed them on long telescoping steel legs that keep the sculptures suspended just a few inches above the water.

Setting Up the Centerpiece

The hummingbird feeding from a trumpet flower is the focal point of the show. The sculpture had to be built in two sections so that it would fit into a truck and through regular doorways. When we set it up, the wings are positioned atop the body, and the steel base that keeps the structure from tipping over is hidden under mulch, dirt, or moss.

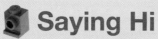 ## Saying Hi

When the exhibit is finally installed, I will often sign autographs, give presentations, talk about how the sculptures are made, and do all kinds of activities together with the guests on opening day.

I always make sure to have a brick building zone set up at my exhibitions so that everyone can get a chance to create something. I hope that, upon seeing my sculptures, people are inspired to construct great things themselves.

Piece by Piece

My premiere New York City solo art exhibition was a show called *Piece by Piece*, which followed the tale of my flight from office life

and explored a collection of work that spanned the serious to the commercial to the zany. It featured larger-than-life classic children's toys and statements on urban transportation and sustainability as well as home products like lamps, wall art, and books.

Setting Up

Installing a 4,000-square-foot art show is a lot of work! Even though all the sculptures were already built and the floor plan and layout were designed months in advance, it still took six of us three full days to set up. There's a lot of precise measuring involved to make sure hanging pieces are level and aligned. Large sculptures need several people to lift and put them in position.

Bicycle Triumphs Traffic

Because I live in New York City, I ride my bike everywhere, and my family doesn't own a car. One morning as I was riding my bike to my studio from my home in Midtown Manhattan, I noticed that in both directions, as far as I could see, traffic was completely stopped and all was silent. The only sound was the pedaling of my bike. As I quietly zipped past everyone in the bike lane, I realized, "I love riding my bike because it doesn't get stuck in traffic!" That was the inspiration for this sculpture.

Help build the **biggest, gnarliest, clogged up** traffic jam in the world!

Sean Kenney lives in New York City and rides his bike every day to get around town. He doesn't own a car, and advocates for reducing traffic and making the street safer and more enjoyable for everyone.

We need you to build tons of crazy cars to help make a huge clogged up traffic jam. Sean will add all your crazy contraptions to the center of his new sculpture, a towering life-size bicycle, showing that **Sean loves riding his bike because it doesn't get stuck in traffic!**

▣ Building It

The sculpture was built at the BrickMagic fan event in
Raleigh, North Carolina. Over the course of two days,
thousands of kids (and adults!) built the world's biggest,
gnarliest, most clogged up traffic jam using over 75,000
black pieces, while I created a life-size eco-green bicycle
triumphing over it all.

There were thousands of crazy cars. I was totally impressed, as everyone's creations were way cooler than I ever could have imagined.

I love that this sculpture is something that not only looks elegant but sends a great message about making smart transportation choices. And best of all, it represents the inspiration and creativity of kids who not only rushed in to help create the crazy traffic jam, but who did so with fervor and excitement. This remains one of my favorite pieces.

Chicago Mall Display

When a new store opened up in Water Tower Place on Chicago's famous Michigan Avenue, I was asked to supply models of renowned Chicago landmarks all built to scale. Unlike most of my models, these were put together entirely unglued! I had to build them solidly enough to survive being trucked from my studio in New York to the store in Chicago. I'm happy to say they made it safely and are now permanently set up in the store's window.

This model of Chicago's second-tallest building is ten feet tall and contains 65,000 pieces. The real building is covered in reflective glass, which made for an incredible challenge in building the model.

Unfortunately, the store owner turned my model of the Tribune Building (above) around so visitors can only see the backside of the building instead of the famous facade with the ornate gothic lettering.

This is Water Tower Place, the building that the store is located in. The model is over six feet tall and has tons of details, like storefronts and parking garages along the first and second floors.

An Eight-Foot Batman

I was asked to help out at a building event hosted by New York City's legendary toy store, FAO Schwarz. Together with over 5,000 kids during the course of three days, we built this gigantic Batman sculpture, designed by Master Builder Steve Gerling (third from left, above).

Sadly, models this large that are built live and unglued can't be moved without falling apart. We had to dismantle the sculpture after the event.

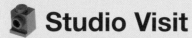

Studio Visit

A few years ago, I opened my studio up for a public "open house," where I welcomed visitors to see works in progress. I talked in detail about how I work, how I organize my studio, and how I design my sculptures. The kids asked great questions.

A fan poses for a quick photo with an autographed poster of my green bike sculpture!

Art and Technology, *Microsoft Gallery, 2009*

The Plasticity of Clay: The Rigidity of Plastic,
LIC Art Center, 2011

In the Place Where We Live, *Gallery M55, 2011*

New York City Art Shows

I enjoy showing my work at art shows in New York City. *Holiday Experience*, left, was a solo show sponsored by ING Bank that opened with an evening of holiday music by a trio featuring Jazz at Lincoln Center's Bryan Carter.

Hong Kong Exhibit

I created several permanent sculptures for a lounge at APM, a chic shopping center in Hong Kong. As part of the unveiling, I traveled to Hong Kong and exhibited some of my other work in addition to the permanent sculptures.

Seven sculptures are permanently installed at APM, so next time you're in Kowloon, go take a look!

LEGO® 父親人像
由2,500顆LEGO® 砌成

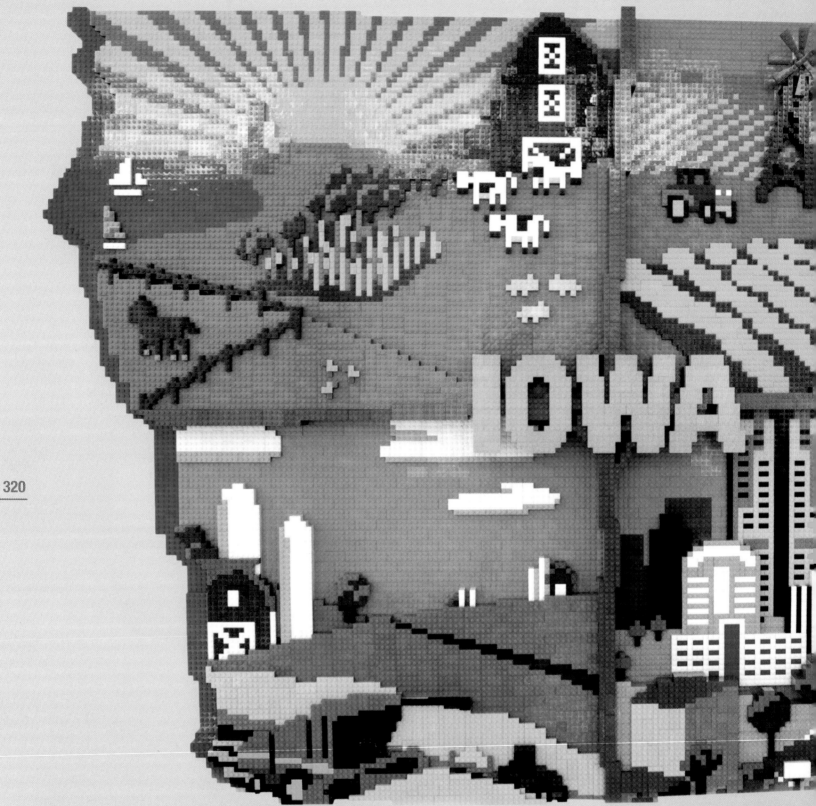

A Map for the Iowa State Fair

This big cartoon map of the state of Iowa divides the state into
quadrants and shows typical farming and urban scenes. The sculpture
is six feet long and was displayed at the Iowa State Fair. The Mississippi

and Missouri rivers, which form the eastern and western borders of the state, are notched out as sunken blue boundaries. Two major interstates separate the quadrants, crossing at a cloverleaf under the raised IOWA block lettering. The sculpture contains almost 30,000 pieces and took nine weeks to design and build. The windmill is my favorite detail.

📦 Book Signings

Most children's book authors who go to bookstores do mainly a reading and a signing. My children's books are all about getting kids inspired to create their own models, so when I host a book signing, I bring bins of pieces to the stores, and together we all build lots of awesome creations before I sign books.

I'm always amazed to see what the kids make. No two creations are ever the same.

324

Wadsworth
Atheneum

Talking to a Crowd

I give a lot of presentations about my work and what I do for a living. What makes my creations special? I talk about how I approach my work and what I think about when deciding how to design my creations. My work has to be uniquely *me* in how I separate myself from the work of others and that of a billion-dollar toy company.

325

LOGO

LOGOS

I've been asked to create a lot of company logos. Many of the logos are hung in office lobbies or conference rooms. Some companies like to use them at trade shows to get people's attention.

Thousands of mini models of the things you can buy on eBay's Gumtree website make up this logo.

328

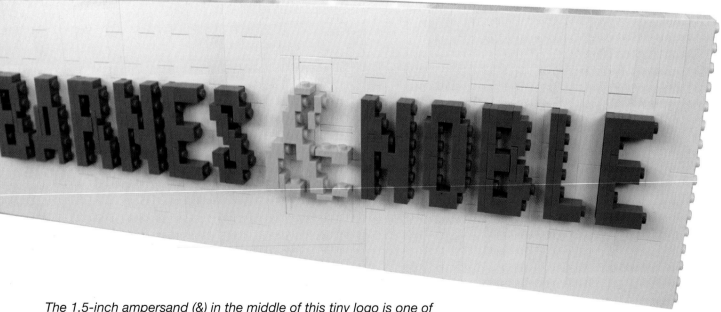

The 1.5-inch ampersand (&) in the middle of this tiny logo is one of the most complicated shapes I've made in such a small space. Can you figure out how I did it?

I hand-carried this logo to Good Morning America's studio in Times Square, and it was used on the live TV show.

This was going to replace the real logo on the cover of a New York magazine issue, but they changed their mind and never printed it!

The Complexity of Simplicity

Did you ever wonder about how a Google search works? It seems so incredibly simple, but if you think about it . . . how did they do that? It's a whirring concoction of amazing technological wizardry. I wanted to create a rendition of Google's logo that, much like Google itself, seemed simple from afar, but upon closer inspection revealed great complexity. I call this model *The Complexity of Simplicity*, because creating something that's easy to use is actually very difficult. This piece is hanging in Google's New York City office.

Big Chase

JPMorgan Chase asked me to create a giant model of their logo at a home-building conference. I created most of the model in my studio beforehand and then shipped it to the show and finished the rest on-site. To acknowledge the theme of the conference, I chose to build a city filled with condos and single-family homes in the middle of the Chase logo.

Cartoon Sculpture

I'm asked to create a lot of flat mosaic logos, but it is always a fun challenge
to make a three-dimensional logo out of a flat two-dimensional drawing.
I like to imagine that the logo is a cartoon drawing of my sculpture,
and then I imagine what that sculpture would have to look like.

This logo, made for tech company Docker, is cute and rendered
well as a bubbly 3-D character. The waves were also a
good challenge to interpret as 3-D shapes;
from the side view, the peaks and
valleys of the waves line up
perfectly with those in the
2-D logo.

I also made some build-it-yourself miniatures that visitors could take with them after seeing the large sculpture in person.

BOOKS

BOOKS

It's a little weird to talk about books in a book, but I was fortunate enough to have had the chance to create eight different children's books.

It's one thing to now have a million pieces to make whatever I want, but when I was a kid, I had a normal-size collection just like most kids today.

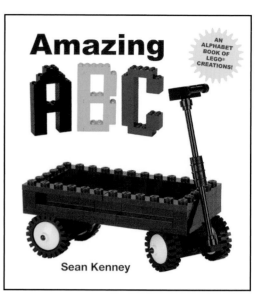

In making these books, I would buy a few retail sets, dump all the parts out and jumble them up, and ask myself, "Okay—what can I make out of these pieces?" I love to use parts in unexpected ways, especially the prefab pieces that look like they can be only one thing. Not the case. A "chair" piece upside down becomes an excavator scooper; sideways it's a fender.

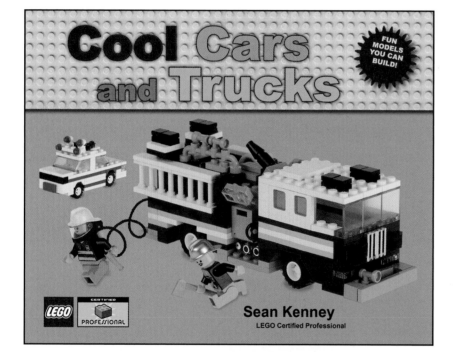

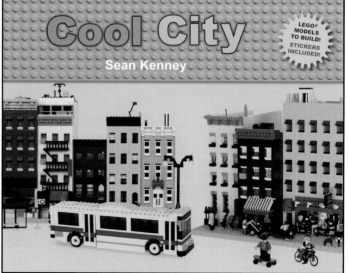

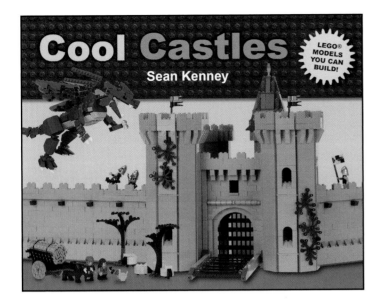

The first step in creating one of these books involves working with my editor, Christy Ottaviano, to come up with a theme or idea. Then, while I plan what specifically will be in the book, Christy works with teams of people at the publishing house to edit all the content, design the book layouts, create the covers, and get the book distributed to bookstores around the world.

With my publisher and editor Christy Ottaviano at one of the book photo shoots

Each book starts out as a storyboard. When I draw these layouts, I think about the models I'd like to design for the book and how I might want to showcase their details, or teach readers about how they're built. The storyboard goes through lots of editing as the book develops. Sometimes after I start designing the model, I realize I might want to show it differently than I'd planned, so I have to go back and make changes to my drawings.

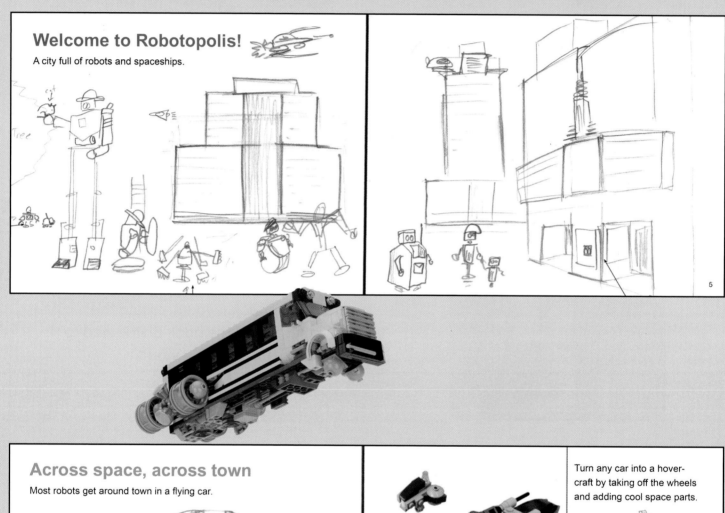

Welcome to Robotopolis!

A city full of robots and spaceships.

5

Across space, across town

Most robots get around town in a flying car.

Use an antennae to connect circles

8

Turn any car into a hover-craft by taking off the wheels and adding cool space parts.

What other kinds of flying cars can you make?

9

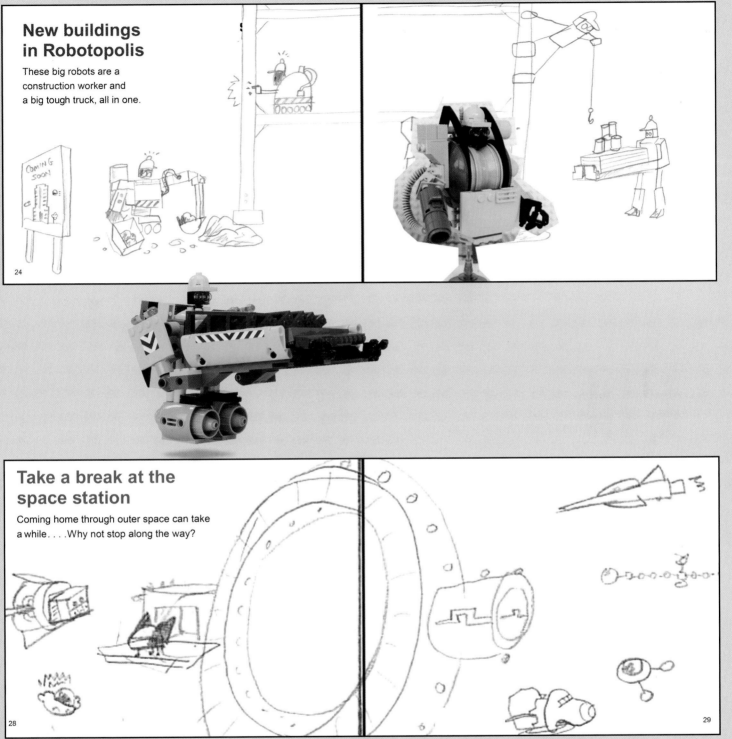

New buildings in Robotopolis

These big robots are a construction worker and a big tough truck, all in one.

24

Take a break at the space station

Coming home through outer space can take a while. . . . Why not stop along the way?

28

29

After I've started building the models, I create a "photo dummy" version of my storyboard, where I take quick pictures of the models and paste them into the layouts. This helps me decide how to pose the models and stage the scenes and helps my publisher and my photographer understand what I'm planning.

The Photo Shoot

Once all the models are built, I transport them to the Manhattan studio of photographer John Barrett. We spend two to three days shooting all the models for a thirty-two-page book. I set up the model in front of the camera, and John controls the camera and lighting so the model looks its best and matches the angles I've planned in my photo dummy.

It's funny that we often have a huge room full of equipment and people just to shoot a one-inch-tall model!

Below, creative director Patrick Collins, photographer John Barrett, publisher and editor Christy Ottaviano, and book designer Elynn Cohen assist in the shoot.

The creative team reviews the photos on computer monitors after every shot to make sure they're perfect!

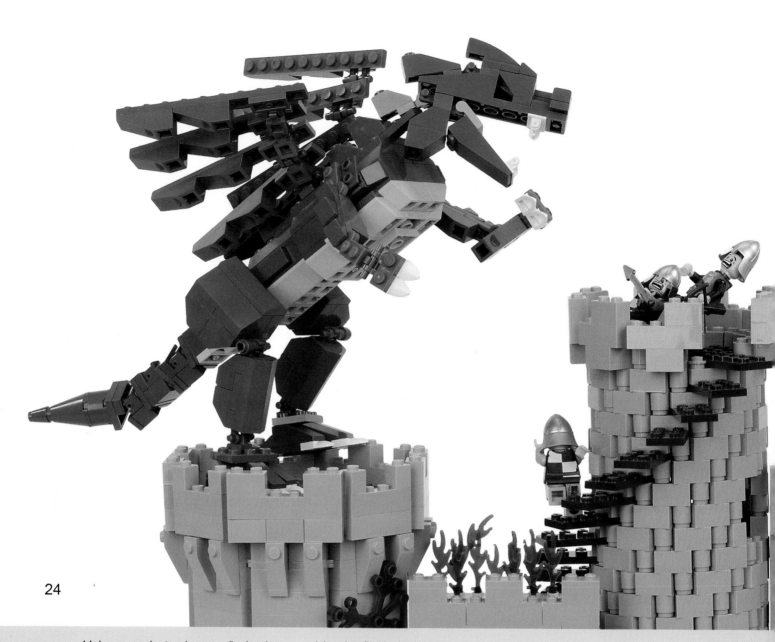

24

Using my photo dummy (below) as a guide, the final photos are placed into the layouts (above).

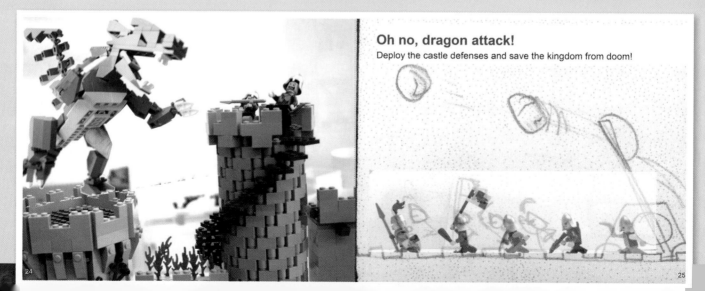

Oh no, dragon attack!
Deploy the castle defenses and save the kingdom from doom!

24

25

Oh no, dragon attack!

Deploy the castle defenses and save the kingdom from doom!

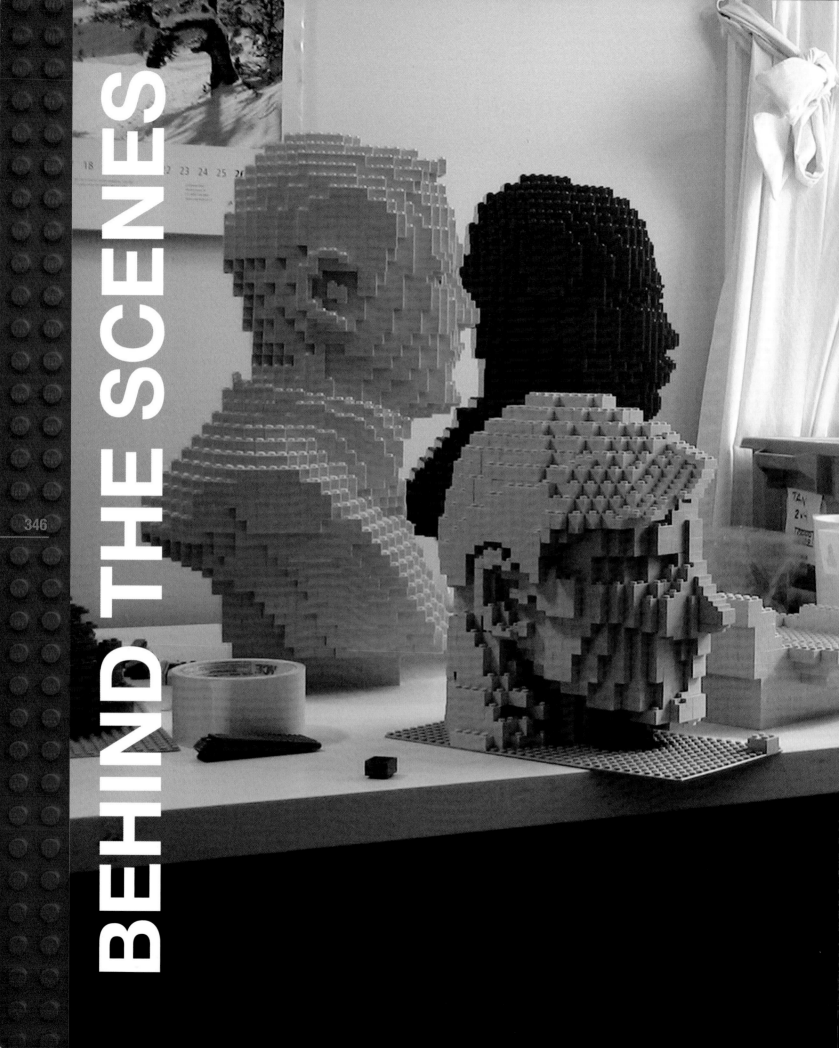

BEHIND THE SCENES

BEHIND THE SCENES

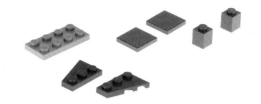

There's no secret to how I build my sculptures—I buy a lot of pieces, design and build things over and over until I get the look right, and then try to learn from my mistakes so that next time I skip the mistakes and do an even better job.

My studio, building exterior (left), lounge and meeting area (right)

Before

After

Welcome to My Studio

I recently moved into a 4,000-square-foot former carriage house in Brooklyn that had a leaky roof and no plumbing, gas, or electricity. I renovated it into a modern open studio space that includes a lounge area, a flexible work space, a wood shop, and a thousand square feet of warehouse-style storage for crated sculptures and millions of pieces.

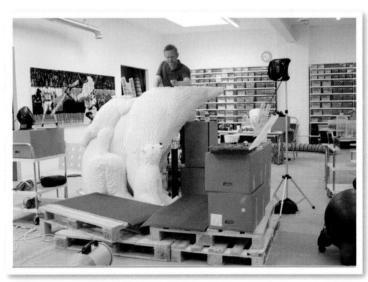

New studio launch party with my editor Christy and both our families.

No Two Days the Same

We rearrange the studio work floor constantly to accommodate all kinds of projects, large and small. Giant sculptures need a lot of space for us to walk around as we work, plus we need space for tool carts and tables and drawings. Smaller projects can be done sitting at a desk (a rare treat for my feet)!

My sculptures always start off as ideas and drawings; I have always loved to draw. All my assistants are artists as well. We research and draw as we explore how to capture the emotion of whatever we are creating.

354

We make plans and schematics for ourselves to follow and then build the sculpture line-by-line, row-by-row, interlocking every piece as we go, for maximum strength. We build beams and grids inside the sculpture to keep the curvy walls straight and to make the sculpture strong (above).

My son, Oliver, tests this structure's load-bearing strength.

For this sculpture, I wanted the baby bears to be cute and playful. My assistant Jung Ah drew these cartoons while watching videos of real polar bears.

After we finish building a sculpture, we photograph it in the studio. The photos are used for my portfolio, my website, marketing, and this book! After we're done, the sculpture is crated up and loaded into a truck for shipment.

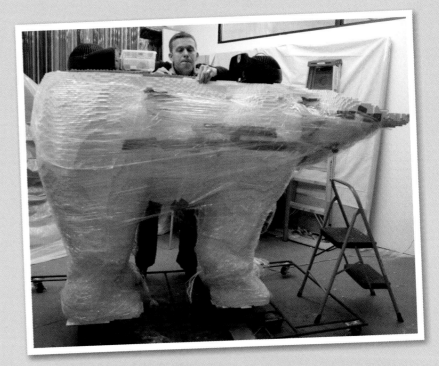

When building sculptures this large, I'll often wrap the completed areas in plastic or paper to protect from bumps or falling glue drops.

356

The legendary John Barrett has photographed a lot of my work; he has the ability to capture the soul of the characters he shoots.

This crate is almost as large as a compact car!

LOOKING UP/OFF/OUTWARDS

Putting Pencil to Paper

A picture is worth a thousand words! My assistants and I make drawings to communicate our ideas to one another. We have to think about how the sculpture will be attached to its base, how large a crate it will need, and many other elements that are external to building the model itself.

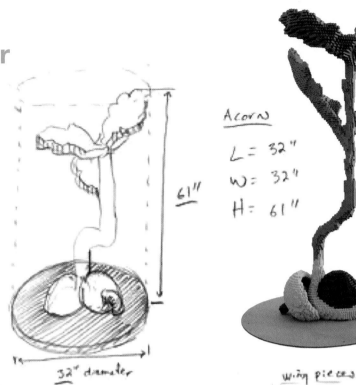

Acorn
L = 32"
W = 32"
H = 61"

61"

32" diameter

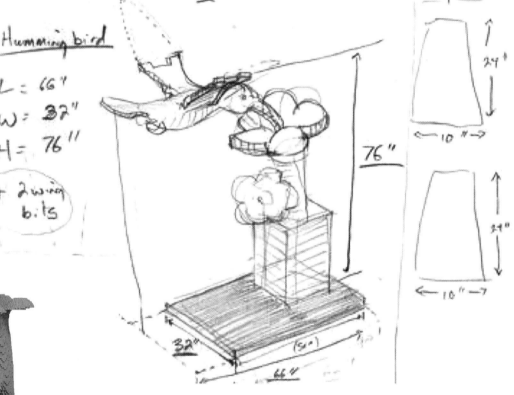

Hummingbird
L = 66"
W = 37"
H = 76"

+ 2 wing bits

76"

32"

66"

wing pieces

24"
←10"→

24"
←10"→

This drawing of my hummingbird sculpture (see also pages 288–289) shows how the upper wings can separate so that the sculpture can fit through a door (and into a smaller crate).

The face-cutout photo op mosaics that I create (see pages 262–263) always start off as hand-drawn cartoons. After I draw the cartoon, I scan it into the computer and then add color using a paint program.

My studio manager, Jen, models a pair of very comfortable pants.

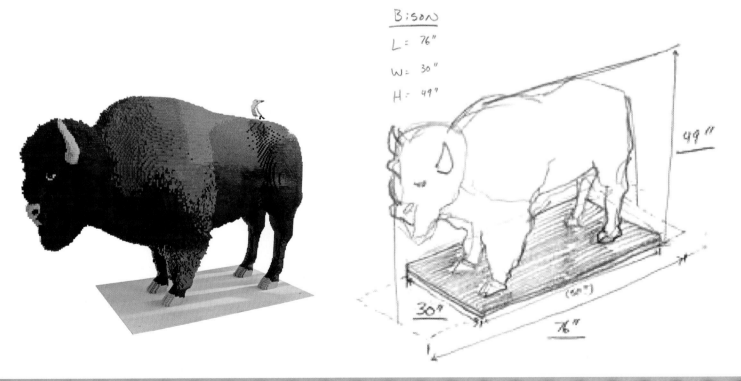

Bison
L = 76"
W = 30"
H = 49"

49"

30"

76"

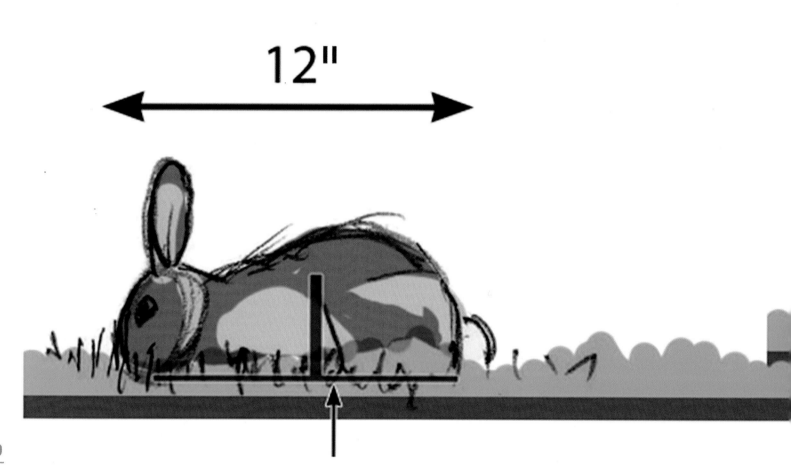

12"

From Proposal to Reality

When I'm proposing a new sculpture or an exhibit, I'll often make drawings like the one above to illustrate to my client what I would like the sculptures to look like. This drawing eventually came to life as the sculptures you see here.

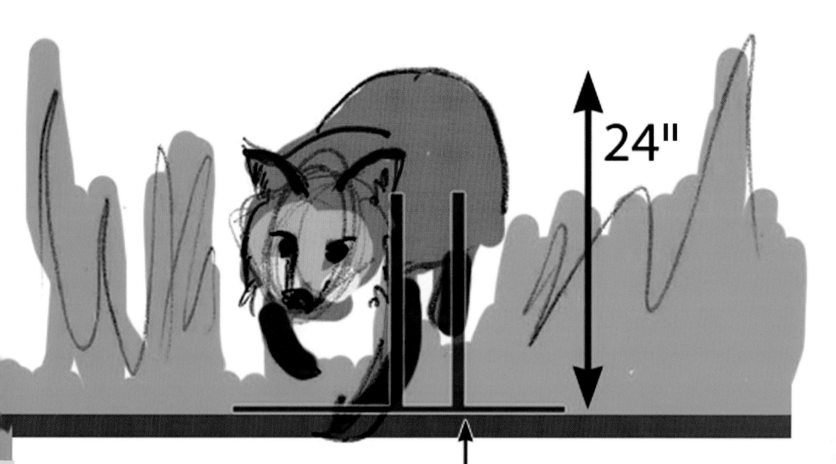

24"

We always spend a lot of time on the faces of the animal sculptures. In this case, I wanted the fox to look cunning and sneaky. This was a prototype I created while working out his expression.

Building a Landmark

This model took two months to design and build together with my assistants Evan and Natsuki. I spent the first two weeks shaking my fist in the air yelling "GUSTAVE!" (convinced that Gustave Eiffel was a crazy lunatic) and the last two weeks shaking my head (convinced he was a crazy genius). Square pieces are good at building straight lines, but everything in the Eiffel Tower sits on angles and diagonals. Building so many diagonal shapes is tricky, and it's even harder when the whole thing needs to be hollow. But it was important to me that you could see straight through the tower's latticework the way you can in real life.

I built a lot of prototypes, drew a lot of drawings, and worked from a lot of photographs until I finally had a plan. I realized after about a week that there were a lot of recurring patterns in the shape of the tower, so I could build a prototype of each section, mark it on the drawing, and then have my assistants build the final multiple glued copies of each prototype.

Crazy math makes me laugh!
Ha-ha!

Many Tries to Get It Right

Creating a human face is one of the hardest assignments any artist can undertake in any medium. There are no shortcuts or tricks—you just have to keep at it until you get it right. I usually build a half prototype (on the raised stool) to get the shape and facial features right, because it's easier to take apart and rework than a full head. Then, when it's to my liking, I build a fully glued copy.

Sketching, Metal, Building

I had only three weeks to build a seven-foot-wide model of the Nintendo DSi for Nintendo's flagship store in Rockefeller Center. I started by taping together a lot of graph paper and drawing a giant model based on measurements of the real DSi. I rush-ordered 50,000 special light blue pieces, and while I waited for them to arrive, I built lots of prototypes and drew out every button, port, screw, and knob.

My welder Haksul created a steel frame based on my drawings, and when the parts arrived, I had only ten days to build it! One of my assistants created the two touchscreen mosaics while I followed my drawings and built the final model around the steel frame. I finished seven hours before the sculpture was unveiled! Whew!

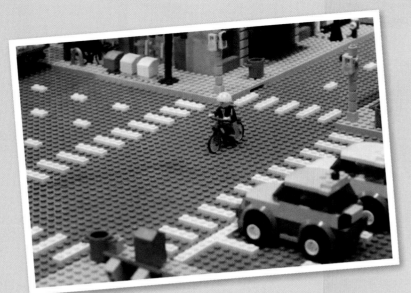

Making a Movie

Together with animator David Pagano and filmmaker Ma Shumin, I set out to create a public service announcement about bicycle safety. We had to build a lot of sets and props for the film, light the scenes properly, and rebuild when we changed camera angles. We filmed the entire thirty-second PSA in four very long days!

You can watch the "Red Light" film online at www.youtube.com/seankenney.

Animator David Pagano,
Director Ma Shumin,
and me.

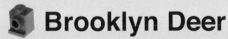 **Brooklyn Deer**

Building really tall sculptures like this life-size buck is difficult because we need to get ourselves high up off the ground, together with our bins of parts and our prototypes and drawings. Above, my assistant Jisun sits on scaffolding with all her tools and parts, while Jung Ah stands on a chair as they work together to get the deer's expression just right.

The North American Brooklyn buck is spotted foraging for taxis in its native habitat. One can tell from its look of consternation it is clearly saying to itself, "You can never get a cab when it's snowing. I should have taken the train."

🧱 Creepy Hanging Sculptures

In creating a sculpture that hangs from the ceiling, we need to make sure it will not list or lean in an unusual way. We usually leave a section of the sculpture hollow so that we can add weights later to balance the body properly. This cute spider worked out pretty well, but after we were done hanging it and had assembled the legs, we couldn't set it down! The legs were so spindly that we had to build a wacky wooden bed for it to rest on (far right).

 **That's a Lot of Pink**

Many people think that I have access to special colors, shapes, or pieces . . . but I don't! I can only get the pieces that you can. Granted, I purchase them in bulk, but the

pieces available to me are the ones currently being made for the kits in stores.

Snow Leopard

I asked my assistant Geoffrey to create a snow leopard
on the prowl to showcase predator/prey relationships as
part of my exhibit *Nature Connects*. Geoffrey watched
a lot of videos and researched photos to get the colors,
pose, and expression just right. He prepared a diagram
for our welders to create an armature and then worked
with some of my other assistants to make sure the snow
leopard's expression was menacing and realistic.

 # Collaboration

I talk a lot in this book about my assistants, and that's because they are a big part of the sculptures that we create. Everything we make is always a collaborative effort and reflects input and ideas from all of us.

I think of myself as a creative director at times and try to offer high-level ideas and a framework in which my team can let their creative muscles grow.

It's important to me that the people on my team are artistically stimulated and having fun. I might have the main premise for what a sculpture could be, or how it might need to come together, but the final product is the result of many creative ideas, sketches, and conversations (and laughs) along the way.

INDEX